SPOTLIGHT

ALBUQUERQUE

ZORA O'NEILL

Contents

ALBUQUERQUE

ALBUQUERQUE

As a tourist destination, Albuquerque may labor in the shadow of the jet-set arts colonies to the north, but as a city, it's a thriving haven for those who pride themselves on being down-to-earth and sensible. If Santa Fe is the "City Different" (a moniker Albuquerqueans razz for its pretentiousness), then New Mexico's largest city, with a population of nearly a million in the greater metro area, is proudly the "City Indifferent," unconcerned with fads, cultivated quirkiness, and flawless facades.

Which is not to say the city doesn't have its pockets of historic charm, well away from the traffic-clogged arteries of I-40 and I-25, which intersect in the center in a graceful tangle of looping, turquoise-trimmed bridges. The Duke City was founded three centuries ago, its cumbersome name that of a Spanish nobleman but its character the product of later eras: the post-1880 downtown district; the University of New Mexico campus, built in the early 20th century by John Gaw Meem, the architect who defined pueblo revival style; and Route 66, the highway that joined Albuquerque to Chicago and Los Angeles in 1926.

Spread out on either side of the Rio Grande, from volcanic mesas on the west to the foothills of the Sandia Mountains along the east, Albuquerque enjoys a striking natural setting. Accessible hiking and biking trails run through diverse environments. In the morning, you can stroll under centuries-old cottonwood trees near the wide, muddy river; in the afternoon, you can hike along the edge of a

HIGHLIGHTS

LOOK FOR ◖ TO FIND RECOMMENDED SIGHTS, ACTIVITIES, DINING, AND LODGING.

◖ **Rio Grande Nature Center State Park:** Savor a bit of country in the city in this bird-filled sanctuary along the river. Hiking and biking trails head north and south along the cottonwood-shaded irrigation channels (page 13).

◖ **KiMo Theater:** A fantasia of Southwestern decorative styles, this former cinema is one of the few examples of pueblo deco style. Now restored and run with city money, it's the showpiece of downtown (page 14).

◖ **Nob Hill:** Hobnob and boutique hop in Albuquerque's quirkiest shopping district, developed in sleek modern style in the 1940s. Sidewalk cafés and bars provide a place to rest up afterward (page 18).

◖ **Sandia Peak Tramway:** Zip up the world's longest single-cable tram to the crest of the mountain that looms over Albuquerque. At the top, you'll get a vertigo-inducing view across the whole metro area and out to the west (page 21).

◖ **Acoma Pueblo:** This windswept village on a mesa west of Albuquerque is one of the oldest communities in the United States. Visit for the views as well as for the delicate black-on-white pottery made only here (page 47).

◖ **Tinkertown Museum:** An enthralling collection of one man's lifetime of whittling projects, this folk-art exhibit is inspiring for adults and a delight for kids (page 54).

© AVALON TRAVEL

◖ **Valles Caldera National Preserve:** In the crater formed by a collapsed volcano, 89,000 acres of grassy valleys are set aside for very controlled public access. You must make reservations to hike here, but it's worth planning for (page 61).

windswept mountain range with views across the vast empty land beyond the city grid. And at the end of the day, you'll see Albuquerque's most remarkable feature, the dramatic light show as the setting sun reflects bright pink off the Sandia (Watermelon) Mountains.

The city is also an excellent (and reasonably priced) base for exploring the many interesting pueblos and natural attractions nearby, and it's just an hour's drive to Santa Fe, with easy day trips or scenic drives through the mountains in between. The main outing is the 65 miles west to Acoma Pueblo, a thousand-year-old settlement atop a natural fortress of stone. In the Manzano Mountains southeast of town lie a series of ruined pueblos, last inhabited during the early years of Conquest. The road that links them also winds past a canyon known for its fall colors and a historic hotel in a distinctly New Mexican style. Naturalists will want to head south to the Bosque del Apache, one of the United States' largest bird sanctuaries, which attracts 15,000 sandhill cranes in November. Drive down before dawn to see the birds at their most active and then wind your way back north via the Quebradas Backcountry Byway, a dirt route through rainbow-striped hills.

Whether you're en route to Santa Fe or just making a day loop, you have several ways to head north. The most direct is I-25, which cuts through dramatic rolling hills; take a short detour to Kasha-Katuwe Tent Rocks National Monument, where pointed white rocks tower above a narrow canyon. Beginning east of Albuquerque, the historic Turquoise Trail winds along the back side of the Sandias, then through the former mining town of Madrid, resettled as an arts colony, with galleries occupying the cabins built against the black, coal-rich hills.

The most roundabout route north is along the Jemez Mountain Trail, a scenic byway northwest of Albuquerque through the brick-red rocks surrounding Jemez Pueblo, then past a number of natural hot springs. The road runs along the edge of Valles Caldera National Preserve, a pristine valley where the daily number of visitors is carefully limited, so you can enjoy the vistas in solitude.

PLANNING YOUR TIME

Because it's not so full of must-see historic attractions, Albuquerque really fares best as the primary focus of a trip, when you have time to enjoy the natural setting and the people. Ideally, you would spend a leisurely week here soaking up a little Route 66 neon, enjoying the downtown entertainment, hiking in the Sandias, taking scenic drives, and bicycling along the Rio Grande.

But it is difficult to recommend more than a couple of days in Albuquerque if you're also planning to visit Santa Fe and Taos in a limited time. In this case, you'll probably want to allocate only two or three days on your way in or out—preferably the latter, because Albuquerque's modern, get-real attitude is best appreciated after you've been in the adobe dreamland of Santa Fe for a bit. Spend a day driving west to Acoma Pueblo, then the next relaxing and knocking around Old Town and the shops in Nob Hill. Or if you prefer a last dose of open sky, take the tramway up to Sandia Peak and hike along the crest trail—at the end of your trip, you'll be able to handle the elevation with no problem.

Any time of year is enjoyable in the city proper—even the winters are mild in the low basin around the river, though the Sandias often get heavy snow. As elsewhere, summer heat is broken by heavy afternoon rainstorms. And because Albuquerque is seldom at the top of tourists' lists, there's never a time when it's unpleasantly mobbed. Hotel prices are highest in summer, but not a dramatic hike from low-season rates.

HISTORY

Even before tourists beat a path to points north, Albuquerque was a way station. It was established in 1706 as a small farming outpost on the banks of the Rio Grande, where Pueblo Indians had been cultivating crops since 1100, and named after a Spanish duke. When the Camino Real, the main trade route north from Mexico, developed decades later, the Villa de San Felipe de Alburquerque (the first "r" was lost over the years) was ideally situated, and the town prospered and soon outgrew its original adobe fortress, the central plaza ringed with one-story haciendas and a church.

Life continued relatively quietly through the transition to U.S. rule in 1848. But in 1880 the railroad came through town—or near enough. The depot was two miles from the main plaza, but investors were quick to construct "New Town," which became the downtown business district. Railroad Avenue (now Central) connected the two communities, though increasingly "Old Town" fell by the wayside, its adobe buildings occupied primarily by the Mexican and Spanish population maintaining their rural lifestyle, while Anglos dominated commerce and the construction of the new city. Developers rapidly built up the land around the train station, with hotels, banks, shops, and more, while other visionaries looked to "the heights"—the sand hills east of the tracks—as the site for a new university.

In the early 20th century, Albuquerque's crisp air was lauded for its beneficial effect on tuberculosis symptoms, and sanatoriums flourished. By 1912, these patients made up nearly a quarter of the state's population. Then Route 66 was laid down Central Avenue in the 1930s. By the next decade, car traffic and business were booming, and by the 1950s, the characteristic neon signage on the numerous motor-court hotels and diners was in place.

Albuquerque's character changed again following World War II, when recruits who had trained at Kirtland Air Force Base returned to settle down. At the same time, the escalating Cold War fueled Sandia National Labs, established in 1949, and engineers relocated to work on defense technology (thanks to the labs, Albuquerque still has more PhDs per capita than any other major city in the United States). Streets were carved into the northeast foothills in anticipation of the tract houses these new workers would inhabit, and over the course of the 1940s, the population exploded from 35,000 to 100,000; by 1959, 207,000 people lived in Albuquerque.

Growth has been steady ever since, and in the 1990s, the city experienced another development boom, helped along by the construction of one of Intel's largest American manufacturing plants. More recently, a growing film industry spurred the construction of Albuquerque Studios, one of the largest production facilities in the country. Subdivisions have spread across the West Mesa, and small outlying communities such as Bernalillo and Placitas have been incorporated into the larger metro area. Now they're primarily wealthy suburbs, though portions, such as Corrales and Los Ranchos de Albuquerque, both in the North Valley along the river, retain a village feel that's not too far from the city's roots as a farming community three centuries back.

ORIENTATION

Albuquerque's greater metro area covers more than 100 square miles, but visitors will likely see only a handful of neighborhoods, all linked by Central Avenue (historic Route 66), the main east–west thoroughfare across town. Visitors typically start in Old Town: The city's best museums are clustered here, a few blocks from the Rio Grande, which runs north–south through the city. East from Old Town lies downtown, where most of the city's bars and clubs are located, along with the bus and train depots. Central Avenue then continues under I-25 and past the University of New Mexico campus. Just east of the school, the Nob Hill shopping district occupies about 10 blocks of Central. After this, the rest of Albuquerque blurs into the broad area known as the Northeast Heights, where there are only a few attractions of note—visitors will want to come up this way, to the farthest edge of the heights, to hike in the foothills and ride the Sandia Peak Tramway to the top of the mountain. The other notable parts of town—technically, separate villages—are Los Ranchos de Albuquerque and Corrales. These are two districts in the North Valley—the stretch of the river north of Central—that contain a few of the city's better lodging options; from Old Town, head north on Rio Grande Boulevard to reach Los Ranchos, then jog west over the river and north again to Corrales.

When you're trying to get your bearings, do as the locals do and keep your eyes on the mountain, along the east side of the city. Street addresses are followed by the city quadrant (NE, NW, SE, SW); Central Avenue forms the dividing line between north and south, while the east–west border is roughly along 1st Street and the train tracks. When locals talk about "the Big I," they mean the relatively central point where I-40 (east–west) and I-25 (north–south) intersect. You won't need to use the freeways for much until you head east to the foothills or west to Petroglyph National Monument.

Sights

To cruise the major attractions in town and get oriented, put yourself in the hands of **ABQ Trolley Co.** (303 Romero St. NW, 505/240-8000, www.abqtrolley.com, Apr.–Oct., $25). Departing from Old Town, the stucco-coated open-sided trolley takes a 75-minute tour through downtown and up to the university and Nob Hill, with fun and informed commentary along the way. The route passes many filming locations for TV shows and movies, as well as Albuquerque Studios, some of the largest such facilities in the United States. The company also offers once-a-month theme tours—such as "Albucreepy," a nighttime tour of supposedly haunted locations, or a pizza crawl—which are extra fun because they draw locals as well. Tickets are cheaper if purchased in advance online, and also give you discounts at restaurants and attractions around town.

OLD TOWN AND THE RIO GRANDE

Until the railroad arrived in 1880, Old Town wasn't old—it was the *only* town, a cluster of one-story haciendas on the riverbank with the formal title of La Villa de San Felipe de Alburquerque. Today, the labyrinthine old adobes have been repurposed as souvenir emporiums and galleries; the city's major museums are nearby on Mountain Road. Despite all the chile-pepper magnets and cheap cowboy hats, the residential areas surrounding the shady plaza retain a strong Hispano flavor, and the historic Old Town buildings have a certain endearing scruffiness—they're lived-in, not polished. Because there are few formal sights but plenty of lore in the neighborhood, the free walking tour with the Albuquerque Museum of Art and History is recommended. A few blocks west of Old Town runs the Rio Grande, a ribbon of green space through the city and a quiet reminder of the city's agricultural history.

Albuquerque BioPark

This kid-friendly park (2601 Central Ave. NW, 505/768-2000, www.cabq.gov/biopark,

9 A.M.–5 P.M. Mon.–Fri., 9 A.M.–6 P.M. Sat. and Sun. June–Aug., 9 A.M.–5 P.M. daily Sept.–May, $7) on the riverbank just west of Old Town contains two components. On one side is an aquarium, with a giant shark tank, a creepy tunnel full of eels, and displays on underwater life from the Gulf of Mexico and up the Rio Grande. The other half is botanical gardens, including a desert hothouse and a butterfly habitat. The most New Mexico–specific installation, and the most interesting, is the 10-acre Rio Grande Heritage Farm, a recreation of a 1930s operation with heirloom apple orchards and rare types of livestock, such as Percheron horses and Churro sheep. It's an idyllic setting near the river and fun for kids (especially if you're there for the apple harvest).

Pay an extra $5, and you also get admission to the **Rio Grande Zoo** (903 10th St. SW), as well as a ride on the miniature train that links the two areas. It's not particularly groundbreaking, but kids can run around among trumpeting elephants and screeching peacocks. The window into the gorilla nursery is probably the most fascinating exhibit. Between the zoo and aquarium, on the east bank of the river, south of Central, so-called **Tingley Beach** (1800 Tingley Dr. SW, sunrise–sunset, free) is 18 acres of paths and ponds for fishing; you can also rent pedal boats and bicycles here.

Albuquerque Museum of Art and History

The museum (2000 Mountain Rd. NW, 505/243-7255, www.cabq.gov/museum, 9 A.M.–5 P.M. Tues.–Sun., $4, free 9 A.M.–1 P.M. Sun.) has a permanent collection ranging from a few choice Taos Society of Artists members (compare Ernest L. Blumenschein's *Star Road and White Sun* with *Acoma Legend,* a painting by his wife, Mary Greene Blumenschein, which use similar colors and allegorical techniques but very different styles) to contemporary work by the likes of Nick Abdalla, whose sensual imagery makes Georgia O'Keeffe's

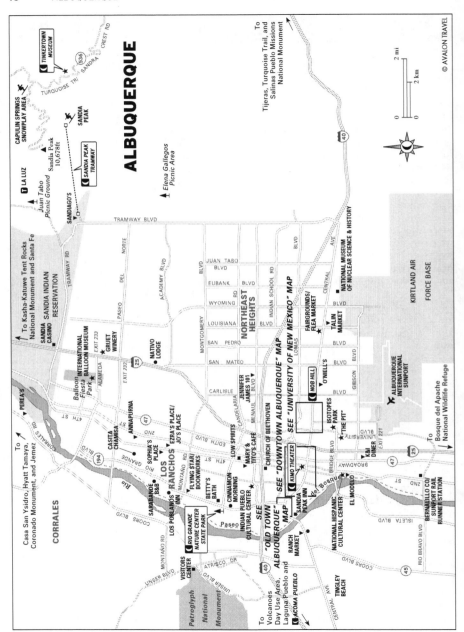

ALBUQUERQUE

TINKERTOWN MUSEUM

CREST RD

TURQUOISE TRL/ SANDIA

536

TURQUOISE TRL

CAPULIN SPRINGS
SNOWPLAY AREA

To
Tijeras, Turquoise Trail, and
Salinas Pueblo Missions
National Monument

To Kasha-Katuwe Tent Rocks
National Monument and Santa Fe

LA LUZ

SANDIA
PEAK

Juan Tabo
Picnic Ground   Sandia Peak
10,678ft

SANDIAGO'S

SANDIA PEAK
TRAMWAY

Elena Gallegos
Picnic Area

TRAMWAY BLVD

40

© AVALON TRAVEL

2 mi

2 km

SANDIA INDIAN
RESERVATION

SANDIA
CASINO

TRAMWAY RD

NORTE

ACADEMY BLVD

DEL

PASEO

JUAN TABO
BLVD

EUBANK   BLVD

WYOMING   RD

NORTE

BLVD

INDIAN SCHOOL RD

BLVD

AVE

CENTRAL

NATIONAL MUSEUM
OF NUCLEAR SCIENCE & HISTORY

KIRTLAND AIR
FORCE BASE

EXIT 233

GRUET
WINERY

INTERNATIONAL
BALLOON MUSEUM

ALAMEDA

EXIT 232

25

NATIVO
LODGE

Balloon
Fiesta Park

PEREA'S

4TH ST

To
Corrales

RD

CORRALES

Casa San Ysidro, Hyatt Tamaya,
Coronado Monument, and Jemez

CORRALES BLVD

Rio
Grande

COORS BLVD

194

RIO GRANDE
BLVD

ANNAPURNA

CASITA
CHAMISA

SOPHIA'S
PLACE

SARABANDE
B&B

MONTAÑO RD

LOS POBLANOS
INN

47

2ND

LOS
RANCHOS

FLYING STAR/
BOOKWORKS

BETTY'S
BATH

CINNAMON
MORNING

INDIAN PUEBLO
CULTURAL CENTER

RIO GRANDE
NATURE CENTER
STATE PARK

Paseo

MONTGOMERY

LOUISIANA

SAN PEDRO

SAN MATEO

CARLISLE

BLVD

BLVD

BLVD

BLVD

BLVD

JENNIFER
JAMES 101

MENAUL BLVD

NORTHEAST
HEIGHTS

CANDELARIA

EDITH BLVD

EZRA'S PLACE/
JO'S PLACE

LOW SPIRITS

4TH ST

MARY &
TITO'S CAFE

CHURCH OF BEETHOVEN

KIMO THEATER

SEE "DOWNTOWN ALBUQUERQUE" MAP

SEE "OLD TOWN
ALBUQUERQUE"
MAP

SANDIA
PEAK INN

EL MODELO

NATIONAL HISPANIC
CULTURAL CENTER

RANCH
MARKET

TINGLEY
BEACH

VISITORS
CENTER

UNSER BLVD

ATRISCO DR

Petroglyph
National
Monument

To
Volcanoes
Day Use Area,
Laguna Pueblo and
ACOMA PUEBLO

CENTRAL   AVE

COORS BLVD

45

RIO BRAVO BLVD

ISLETA BLVD

BERNALILLO CO/
SUNPORT RAIL
RUNNER STATION

2ND   ST

del Bosque

BROADWAY

KAI
DINER

47

25

EXIT 221

BLVD

To
Bosque del Apache
National Wildlife Refuge

UNIVERSITY

BLVD

ALBUQUERQUE
INTERNATIONAL
SUNPORT

GIBSON BLVD

SEE "UNIVERSITY OF NEW MEXICO" MAP

NOB HILL

O'NIELL'S

ISOTOPES
PARK

THE PIT

LOMAS

BLVD

TALIN
MARKET

FAIRGROUNDS/
FLEA MARKET

BRIDGE BLVD

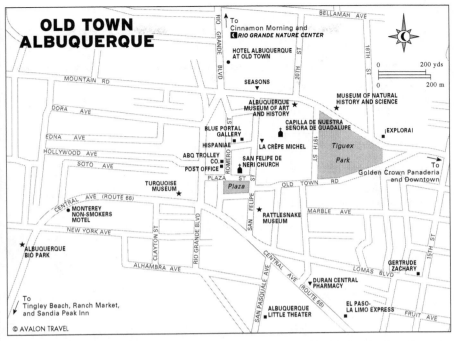

OLD TOWN ALBUQUERQUE

To Cinnamon Morning and
RIO GRANDE NATURE CENTER

HOTEL ALBUQUERQUE
AT OLD TOWN

SEASONS

ALBUQUERQUE
MUSEUM OF ART
AND HISTORY

MUSEUM OF NATURAL
HISTORY AND SCIENCE

BLUE PORTAL
GALLERY

CAPILLA DE NUESTRA
SEÑORA DE GUADALUPE

EXPLORA

HISPANIAE

LA CRÊPE MICHEL

Tiguex
Park

ABQ TROLLEY
CO.

SAN FELIPE DE
NERI CHURCH

To
Golden Crown Panaderia
and Downtown

POST OFFICE

TURQUOISE
MUSEUM

Plaza

OLD TOWN RD

MONTEREY
NON-SMOKERS
MOTEL

CENTRAL AVE (ROUTE 66)

NEW YORK AVE

RATTLESNAKE
MUSEUM

MARBLE AVE

ALBUQUERQUE
BIO PARK

GERTRUDE
ZACHARY

ALHAMBRA AVE

LOMAS BLVD

DURAN CENTRAL
PHARMACY

To
Tingley Beach, Ranch Market,
and Sandia Peak Inn

EL PASO-
LA LIMO EXPRESS

ALBUQUERQUE
LITTLE THEATER

FRUIT AVE

BELLAMAH AVE

MOUNTAIN RD

DORA AVE

EDNA AVE

HOLLYWOOD AVE

SOTO AVE

0   200 yds
0   200 m

© AVALON TRAVEL

flower paintings look positively literal. The history wing covers four centuries, with emphasis on Spanish military trappings, Mexican cowboys, and Albuquerque's early railroad years. Free guided tours run daily around the sculpture garden, or you can join the informative Old Town walking tour (11 A.M. Tues.–Sun. mid-Mar.–mid-Dec.).

American International Rattlesnake Museum

You'd never guess this small storefront just off the plaza (202 San Felipe St. NW, 505/242-6569, www.rattlesnakes.com, 10 A.M.–6 P.M. Mon.–Sat., 1–5 P.M. Sun. June–Aug., $5) houses the largest collection of live snakes in the world, as you have to wade through an enormous gift shop full of plush snakes, wood snakes, little magnet snakes, and snakes on T-shirts to see the real critters. You'll also see some fuzzy tarantulas and big desert lizards, and the reptile-mad staff are usually showing off some animals outside

to help educate the phobic. In the off-season, September–May, weekday hours are 11:30 A.M.–5:30 P.M. (weekends are the same).

Capilla de Nuestra Señora de Guadalupe

Tucked away in a side alley off the main street, this tiny adobe chapel (404 San Felipe St. NW) is dedicated to the first saint of Mexico; her image dominates the wall facing the entrance. The dimly lit room, furnished only with heavy carved seats against the walls, is still in regular use, and the air is sweet with the smell of votive candles and *milagros* placed at Mary's feet and on the modest altar, along with prayers and testimonies. Even at this small scale, the building follows the scheme of many traditional New Mexican churches, with a clerestory that allows sunlight to shine down on the altar.

¡Explora!

This 50,000-square-foot complex adjacent to

UP, UP, AND AWAY: ALBUQUERQUE'S HOT-AIR BALLOON HISTORY

How did it come to be that one of the most iconic sights in Albuquerque is a 127-foot-tall Mr. Peanut figure floating in front of the Sandias? The city's air currents were discovered to be friendly to balloons for the first time in 1882. That was when an adventurous bartender piloted a hydrogen-filled craft into the sky as part of the New Town's Fourth of July celebrations, much to the delight of the assembled crowd, which had waited almost two days for *The City of Albuquerque,* as the balloon was dubbed, to fill. "Professor" Park Tassell, the showman pilot, went aloft alone and landed successfully; the only mishap was that a ballast sandbag was emptied on a spectator's head.

It took another 90 years before Albuquerque again drew attention as a place to pursue this gentle sport – in 1972, the first balloon fiesta was held, with 13 aircraft participating. The gathering, centered around a single race, was organized by a local balloon club as a publicity stunt for a local radio station's 50th-anniversary celebrations. The spectacle drew 20,000 people, most of whom had never even seen a hot-air balloon before – but within a few short years, the event was internationally renowned.

Albuquerque, it turns out, enjoys the world's most perfect weather for navigating hot-air balloons. A phenomenon called the "Albuquerque Box," created by the steep mountains adjacent to the low river bottom, enables pilots to move at different speeds at different altitudes, and even to backtrack if necessary. Combine that with more than 300 days of sunshine per year, and it's no wonder that now more than 700 balloons – including "special shapes" such as Mr. Peanut – convene annually to show off their colors and compete in precision flying contests.

the natural history museum (1701 Mountain Rd. NW, 505/224-8300, www.explora.us, 10 A.M.–6 P.M. Mon.–Sat., noon–6 P.M. Sun., adults $8, children $4) is dedicated to thrilling—and educating—children. Grown-ups may learn something too. Its colorful geodesic-dome top sets a circuslike tone, and inside, more than 250 interactive exhibits demonstrate the scientific principles behind everything from high-wire balancing to optical illusions. Kids can even build robots using Lego systems, and, since this is the desert, a whole section is dedicated to water.

Indian Pueblo Cultural Center

Just north of I-40 from Old Town, the Indian Pueblo Cultural Center (2401 12th St. NW, 505/843-7270, www.indianpueblo.org, 9 A.M.–5 P.M. daily, $6) is a must-visit before heading to any of the nearby Indian communities. The horseshoe-shaped building (modeled after the Pueblo Bonito ruins in Chaco Canyon in northwestern New Mexico) houses a large museum that traces the history of the first settlers along the Rio Grande, depicting the Spanish Conquest as a faintly absurd enterprise. It's illustrated with some beautiful artifacts and showcases the best craftwork from each pueblo. The central plaza hosts dance performances (11 A.M. and 2 P.M. Apr.–Oct., noon Nov.–Mar.), one of the only places to see them outside of the pueblos themselves. The extensively stocked gift shop is a very good place to buy pottery and jewelry; you can also have a lunch of *posole* and frybread at the Pueblo Harvest Café. Don't miss the south wing, which contains a gallery for contemporary art. At the information desk, check on ceremony schedules and get directions to the various pueblos.

Museum of Natural History and Science

This large exhibit space (1801 Mountain Rd. NW, 505/841-2800, www.nmnaturalhistory.org, 9 A.M.–5 P.M. daily) contains

COURTESY ALBUQUERQUE CVB / © MARBLESTREETSTUDIO.COM

Hang out with dinosaurs at the Museum of Natural History and Science.

three major attractions: a planetarium and observatory; a wide-format theater screening the latest vertigo-inducing nature documentaries; and a presentation of Earth's geological history. The geology section is structured as a walk-through time line, beginning with the Big Bang (rendered with black lights and thunderclaps) and meandering through the prehistoric era and age of volcanic activity. Some of the attractions, such the hokey "evolator" time machine, don't live up to the hype, but there's plenty of space given to the crowd-pleasers: dinosaurs. New Mexico has been particularly rich soil for paleontologists, and several of the most interesting finds are on display, such as *Coelophysis* and *Pentaceratops*. In addition, the *Startup* exhibit details the early history of the personal computer, in Albuquerque and elsewhere. The show was funded by former Duke City resident Paul Allen, who founded Microsoft here with Bill Gates, *then* moved to Seattle. Admission is $7 to the main exhibit space or the planetarium and $10 for the theater,

though there are discounts if you buy tickets to more than one.

◖ Rio Grande Nature Center State Park

Familiarize yourself with river ecology at this green haven in the center of town (2901 Candelaria St. NW, 505/344-7240, www.rgnc.org, 8 A.M.–5 P.M. daily, $3/car). You enter the sleek, concrete visitors center (10 A.M.–5 P.M. daily) through a drainage culvert. Beyond an exhibit on water conservation and river ecology, a comfortable glassed-in "living room" lets you watch birds on the pond from the comfort of a lounge chair, with the outdoor sounds piped in through speakers. Outside, you can walk several paved trails across the old irrigation channels and along the river, all shaded by towering cottonwood trees. In the spring and fall, the area draws all manner of migrating birdlife; borrow binoculars from the staff if you want to scout on your own, or join one of the frequent nature walks (including full-moon tours) that take place year-round.

© ZORA O'NEILL

entrance to Rio Grande Nature Center State Park

San Felipe de Neri Church

Established in 1706 along with the city itself, San Felipe de Neri Church (2005 N. Plaza St. NW) was originally built on what would become the west side of the plaza—but it dissolved in a puddle of mud after a strong rainy season in 1792. The replacement structure, on the north side of the plaza, has fared much better, perhaps because its walls, made of adobe-like *terrones* (sun-dried bricks cut out of sod) are more than five feet thick. As they have for two centuries, local parishioners attend Mass here, conducted three times a day, once in Spanish.

Like many religious structures in the area, San Felipe de Neri received a makeover from Eurocentric Bishop Jean Baptiste Lamy of Santa Fe in the second half of the 19th century. Under his direction, the place got its wooden folk Gothic spires, as well as new Jesuit priests from Naples, who added such non-Spanish details as the gabled entrance and the widow's walk. The small yet grand interior has brick floors, a baroque gilt altar, and an elaborate pressed-tin ceiling with Moorish geometric patterns.

A tiny museum (9 A.M.–5 P.M. Mon.–Fri., 10 A.M.–3 P.M. Mon.–Sat., free) on the east side contains some historic church furnishings.

Turquoise Museum

This modest-looking place in a strip mall (2107 Central Ave. NW, 505/247-8650, 10 A.M.–4 P.M. Mon.–Fri., 10 A.M.–3 P.M. Sat., $4) is much more substantial than it looks. It's not just a museum, but also a consumer's resource. Exhibits present the geology and history of turquoise, along with legendary trader J. C. Zachary's beautiful specimens from all over the world. But most folks can't help but think how this relates to all the jewelry they plan to buy. So come here to learn the distinction between "natural" and "real" turquoise and otherwise arm yourself for the shopping ahead.

DOWNTOWN

Once known as bustling New Town, the downtown area of Albuquerque, stretching along Central Avenue between the train tracks and Marquette Avenue, was the city's commercial center, crowded with mule-drawn streetcars, bargain hunters, and wheeler-dealers from the East Coast. Then, in the 1950s and 1960s, shopping plazas in Nob Hill and the Northeast Heights drew business away. By the 1970s, downtown was a wasteland of government office buildings that was utterly desolate after 5 P.M. But thanks to an aggressive urban-renewal scheme initiated in 2000, the neighborhood has regained some of its old vigor, and Central is now a thoroughfare best known for its bars and lounges. By day, you won't see too many specific attractions, but a stroll around reveals an interesting hodgepodge of architectural styles from Albuquerque's most optimistic era. At Central Avenue and 4th Street, two versions of Route 66 intersect. When the original highway was commissioned in 1926, the road from Chicago to the West Coast ran along 4th Street; after 1937, the route was smoothed so that it ran east–west along Central.

KiMo Theater

Albuquerque's most distinctive building is

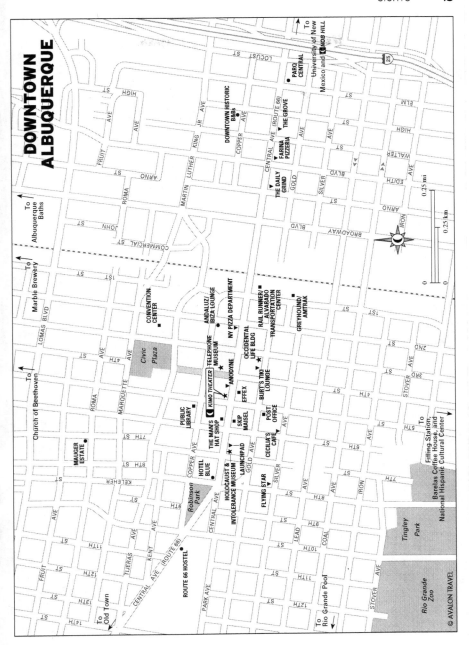

DOWNTOWN ALBUQUERQUE

To University of New Mexico and KNOB HILL
PARQ CENTRAL
DOWNTOWN HISTORIC B&Bs
THE GROVE
FARINA PIZZERIA
CENTRAL AVE (ROUTE 66)
THE DAILY GRIND
To Albuquerque Baths
To Marble Brewery
CONVENTION CENTER
ANDALUZ/ IBIZA LOUNGE
NY PIZZA DEPARTMENT
OCCIDENTAL LIFE BLDG
RAIL RUNNER/ ALVARADO TRANSPORTATION CENTER
GREYHOUND/ AMTRAK
Civic Plaza
TELEPHONE MUSEUM
KIMO THEATER
ANODYNE
EFFEX
BURT'S TIKI LOUNGE
To Church of Beethoven
PUBLIC LIBRARY
THE MAN'S HAT SHOP
SKIP MAISEL
POST OFFICE
MAUGER ESTATE
HOTEL BLUE
LAUNCHPAD
CECILIA'S CAFE
HOLOCAUST & INTOLERANCE MUSEUM
FLYING STAR
Robinson Park
CENTRAL AVE (ROUTE 66)
ROUTE 66 HOSTEL
To Old Town
Tingley Park
Rio Grande Zoo
Filling Station, Barelas Coffee House, and National Hispanic Cultural Center
To Rio Grande Pool
Rio Grande Pool

0   0.25 mi
0   0.25 km

© AVALON TRAVEL

NEW LIFE FOR "NEW TOWN"?

Long a district of desolate concrete plazas and boarded-up shops on windblown streets, Albuquerque's downtown has taken on a new look since 2000. The city has invested more than $350 million in a grand scheme to restore the area to its early-20th-century role as New Town, the hub of Albuquerque's commercial life.

Using the principles of New Urbanism, downtown is now a mixed-use neighborhood where residents can live, work, and play without relying on cars – ideally, everything residents need, from bars to grocery stores, should be within a 10-minute walk. The city built a public-transport hub – including a commuter-rail line – and the chalk dust was blown out of the old Albuquerque High School just east of the railroad tracks on Central Avenue (the micro-neighborhood dubbed "EDo," short for "east downtown") to make chic lofts.

But for all the energy and activity, downtown still lacks one basic: a grocery store. As of 2011, yet another plan for one was in the works, but until it materializes, downtowners have to get in their dreaded cars to stock up elsewhere, or plan carefully around the once-weekly farmers market.

Meanwhile, downtown is facing competition from a new megadevelopment that could be described as "New Suburbanist": The 13,000-acre Mesa del Sol community, on the south side of·the city near the airport, is laid out so that no home is more than 800 yards from groceries. Mesa del Sol's standalone houses are much more familiar to Westerners than downtown's apartments, so this might prove the more popular car-free option.

---

the KiMo Theater (423 Central Ave. NW, 505/768-3522 or 505/768-3544 event info, www.cabq.gov/kimo). In 1927, local businessman and Italian immigrant Carlo Bachechi hired Carl Boller, an architect specializing in movie palaces, to design this marvelously ornate building. Boller was inspired by the local adobe and native culture to create a unique style dubbed "pueblo deco"—a flamboyant treatment of Southwestern motifs, in the same vein as Moorish- and Chinese-look cinemas of the same era. The tripartite stucco facade is encrusted with ceramic tiles and Native American iconography (including a traditional Navajo symbol that had not yet been completely appropriated by the Nazi Party when the KiMo was built). To get the full effect, you must tour the interior to see the cow-skull sconces and murals of pueblo life; enter through the business office just west of the ticket booth (11 A.M.–8 P.M. Wed.–Sat., 11 A.M.–3 P.M. Sun.).

Occidental Life Building

On Gold Avenue at 3rd Street, this one-story office building is another of Albuquerque's gems. With its curlicued facade of white ceramic tile, the ornate 1917 construction looks like the Doge's Palace in Venice rendered in marshmallow fluff. After a 1933 fire, the reconstructing architects added even more frills, such as the crenellations along the top. The entire building is surfaced in white terra-cotta; the tiles were made in a factory in Denver, which sprayed the ceramic glaze onto concrete blocks, each individually molded and numbered, and the blocks were then assembled in Albuquerque according to an overall plan.

Miscellaneous Museums

Production value is low at the storefront **Holocaust & Intolerance Museum** (616 Central Ave. SW, 505/505/247-0606, 11 A.M.–3 P.M. Tues.–Sat., free), but the message is still compelling. Displays cover not just World War II, but also the Armenian genocide and actions against Native Americans. The surprisingly detailed three-story **Telephone Museum** (110 4th St. NW, 505/841-2932, 10 A.M.–3 P.M. Mon., Wed., and Fri., $2) has limited opening hours but is worth a visit if you're there at the right time. For a more modern outlook, visit gallery–art center **516 Arts** (516 Central Ave. SW, 505/242-1445, noon–5 P.M. Tues.–Sat.), which displays often conceptual work by Western artists.

THE UNIVERSITY AND NOB HILL

The state's largest university, another by-product of the railroad boom, was established in 1889 as a tiny outpost on the far side of the tracks. By 1909, under the guidance of its president William George Tight, it had acquired the outline of its distinctive pueblo-inspired architecture (though Tight was then fired, in part for his non–Ivy League aesthetics). Pueblo revival pioneer John Gaw Meem carried on the vision through the 1940s, and even

with contemporary structures now interspersed among the original halls, it's still a remarkably harmonious vision, uniting the pastoral sanctuary feel of the great Eastern campuses with a soothing, minimalist interpretation of native New Mexican forms.

Surrounding the campus is the typical scrum of cheap pizza places, bohemian coffeehouses, and dilapidated bungalow rentals. The next neighborhood east along Central is the city's best shopping district, Nob Hill, developed around a shopping plaza in the late 1940s and still showing that decade's distinctive style in marquees and shop facades.

The University of New Mexico

Nearly 25,000 students use this campus, which sprawls for blocks beyond the old core bounded

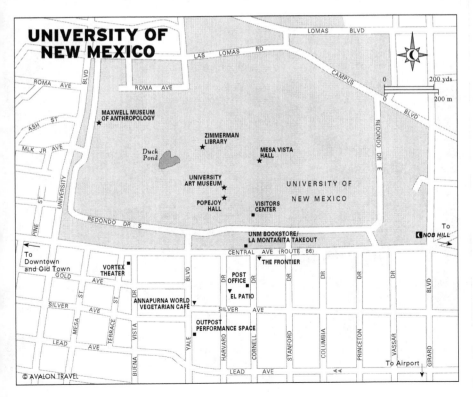

by Central Avenue and University Boulevard. Visitors can park in a complex just inside the UNM campus across from Cornell Street. The info center, where you can pick up a detailed map, is in the southwest corner of the structure. Just across the way, the **University Art Museum** (505/277-4001, 10 A.M.–4 P.M. Tues.–Fri., 1–4 P.M. Sat. and Sun., $5 donation) displays treasures from the permanent fine art collection of more than 30,000 pieces from all over the globe.

Wandering around the grounds, you'll see such classic Meem buildings as **Mesa Vista Hall** (now the Student Services Building) and **Zimmerman Library.** Rest up at the bucolic duck pond, then head for the **Maxwell Museum of Anthropology** (off University Blvd., north of M. L. K. Jr. Blvd., 505/277-4405, 10 A.M.–4 P.M. Tues.–Sat., free), a Meem building designed as the student union. The museum has a particularly good overview of Southwestern Indian culture and a collection of Native American artifacts from university-sponsored digs all over the state.

Nob Hill

Gates trimmed in neon mark the Nob Hill district on Central Avenue at Girard Street and at Washington Boulevard. The area began to grow after 1937, when Route 66 was rejiggered to run along Central. The Nob Hill Shopping Plaza, at Central and Carlisle, signaled the neighborhood's success when it opened as the glitziest shopping district in town a decade later. The area went through a slump from the 1960s through the mid-1980s, but it's again lined with brightly painted facades and neon signs, a lively district where the quirk factor is high—whether you want to buy designer underwear or an antique Mexican mask, you'll find it here. Head off of Central on Monte Vista and keep an eye out for the **Bart Prince house** (3501 Monte Vista Blvd. NE), the home and studio of one of the city's most celebrated contemporary architects, whose favorite forms seem to be spaceships and antennas—it's the residential counterpart to the eccentric businesses that flourish in this area.

Local architect Bart Prince isn't a fan of right angles.

ROUTE 66 GETS A MAKEOVER

Route 66 is one of the biggest repositories of American nostalgia, a little neon ribbon of cool symbolizing the country's economic growth in the 20th century. But the "mother road," on which so many Dust Bowl refugees made their way west and so many beatniks got into their grooves, officially no longer exists. The highway was decommissioned in 1985. Sure, you can still follow the brown historic-marker signs from Chicago to Los Angeles, but in Albuquerque, I-40 bypasses Central Avenue, the old Route 66, and the transient-friendly businesses that once thrived there.

Now those businesses – especially the numerous 1940s motel courts – are derelict and have become hot spots for drug deals and other unsavory business. As part of Albuquerque's aggressive urban-renewal program, city planners demolished a number of hotels, leaving dead neon signs standing like tombstones amid the rubble. But the city had a change of heart with the 1939 De Anza, on the east edge of Nob Hill, and bought it in 2003 to protect, among other things, beautiful interior murals by American Indian painters.

In the meantime, Burqueños have developed fresh affection for their neon-lit heritage. So when the owner of the El Vado Motel, near Old Town, threatened his vintage property with the wrecking ball, the city bought that too. Plans for redevelopment on both properties have stalled repeatedly, but these icons of Route 66 history are worth keeping an eye on.

ALBUQUERQUE METRO AREA

Beyond the neighborhoods described in the previous pages, Albuquerque is a haze of modern tract houses and shopping centers built during the 1960s and later—decades dubbed Albuquerque's "Asphalt Period" by an unkind local journalist. A few sights, particularly along the edges of the city, are well worth seeking out, however.

National Hispanic Cultural Center

Just south of downtown (but not within walking distance) on 4th Street in the historic, and historically neglected, neighborhood of Barelas, this modern complex (1701 4th St. SW, 505/246-2261, www.nhccnm.org, 10 A.M.–5 P.M. Tues.–Sun., $3, free on Sun.) lauds the cultural contributions of Spanish speakers the world over. It has had a huge positive influence in this down-at-the-heels district (even the McDonald's across the street mimics its architecture, but numerous houses—occupied by Hispanics, no less—were demolished for its construction. One woman refused the buyout. She has since died, but her two small houses still sit in the parking lot—almost like an exhibit of their own, representing the larger determination of New Mexican Hispanics to hang on to their land through the centuries.

The central attraction is the museum, which shows work ranging from the traditional santos and *retablos* by New Mexican craftspeople (including Luis Barela, grandson of legendary Taos *santero* Patrocinio Barela) to contemporary painting, photography, and even furniture by artists from Chile, Cuba, Argentina, and more. The best time to visit is on Sunday, when the *torreón* (tower) is open (noon–4 P.M.) to show Frederico Vigil's amazing fresco *Mundos de mestizaje*, a decade-long project depicting the many strands—Arab, Celtic, African—that have contributed to Hispanic culture today. Adjacent to the museum is the largest Hispanic genealogy library in existence, as well as the giant Roy E. Disney Center for Performing Arts.

National Museum of Nuclear Science & History

This spiffy museum (601 Eubank Blvd. SE, 505/245-2137, www.nuclearmuseum.org, 9 A.M.–5 P.M. daily, $8) covers everything you wanted to know about the atomic era, from the development of the weapon on through current

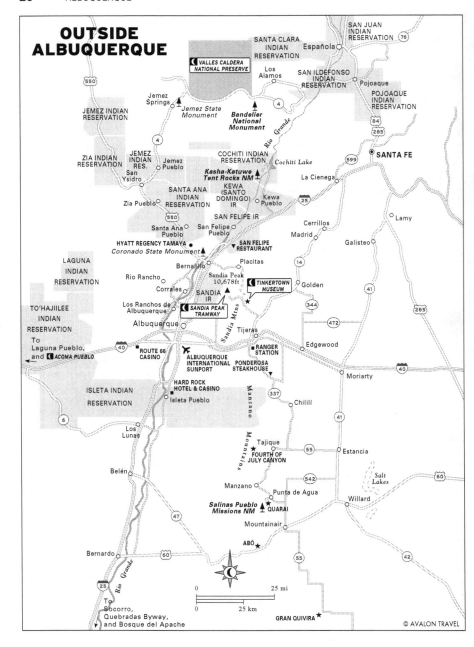

OUTSIDE ALBUQUERQUE

VALLES CALDERA NATIONAL PRESERVE

JEMEZ INDIAN RESERVATION

Jemez Springs

Jemez State Monument

SANTA CLARA INDIAN RESERVATION

SAN JUAN INDIAN RESERVATION

Española

Los Alamos

SAN ILDEFONSO INDIAN RESERVATION

Pojoaque

POJOAQUE INDIAN RESERVATION

Bandelier National Monument

Rio Grande

ZIA INDIAN RESERVATION

JEMEZ INDIAN RES.

Jemez Pueblo

San Ysidro

COCHITI INDIAN RESERVATION

Cochiti Lake

SANTA FE

Kasha-Katuwe Tent Rocks NM

La Cienega

Zia Pueblo

SANTA ANA INDIAN RESERVATION

KEWA (SANTO DOMINGO) IR

Kewa Pueblo

Lamy

Santa Ana Pueblo

SAN FELIPE IR

San Felipe Pueblo

Cerrillos

Madrid

Galisteo

HYATT REGENCY TAMAYA
Coronado State Monument

SAN FELIPE RESTAURANT

LAGUNA INDIAN RESERVATION

Bernalillo

Placitas

Rio Rancho

Sandia Peak 10,678ft

TINKERTOWN MUSEUM

Golden

Corrales

SANDIA IR

TO'HAJIILEE INDIAN RESERVATION

Los Ranchos de Albuquerque

SANDIA PEAK TRAMWAY

Albuquerque

Sandia Mtns

Tijeras

To Laguna Pueblo, and ACOMA PUEBLO

RANGER STATION

Edgewood

ROUTE 66 CASINO

ALBUQUERQUE INTERNATIONAL SUNPORT

PONDEROSA STEAKHOUSE

Moriarty

HARD ROCK HOTEL & CASINO

ISLETA INDIAN RESERVATION

Isleta Pueblo

Manzano

Chililí

Los Lunas

Mountains

Tajique

FOURTH OF JULY CANYON

Estancia

Salt Lakes

Belén

Manzano

Punta de Agua

Willard

Salinas Pueblo Missions NM

QUARAI

Mountainair

ABÓ

Bernardo

GRAN QUIVIRA

Rio Grande

To Socorro, Quebradas Byway, and Bosque del Apache

0   25 mi

0   25 km

© AVALON TRAVEL

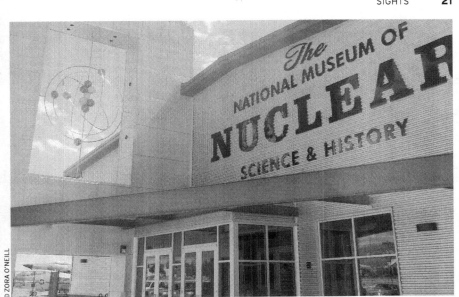

Learn all about the atomic age at Albuquerque's National Museum of Nuclear Science & History.

energy issues. Exhibits cover the ghastly elements of the atomic bomb, but also wonky tech details (check out the display of decoders, set in suitcases for emergency deployment) and pop-culture artifacts, such as "duck and cover" films from the Cold War. Don't miss the beautiful posters by Swiss-American artist Erik Nitsche.

Sandia Peak Tramway

The longest tramway of its type in the world, the tram (505/856-7325, www.sandiapeak. com, $1 parking, $20 round-trip, $12 one-way) whisks passengers 2.7 miles along a continuous line of Swiss-made cables, from Albuquerque's northeast foothills 4,000 feet up to the crest in about 15 minutes. If the wind is blowing, the ride can be a bit alarming—or thrilling, depending on your outlook. The service runs frequently all year-round (9 A.M.–9 P.M. daily June–Aug., 9 A.M.–8 P.M. Wed.–Mon., 5–8 P.M. Tues. Sept.–May), making it a convenient way to get to the ski area; in the summer, you can ride up to the peak, then hike along the crest a few miles to the visitors center.

At the base of the tram, there's a small free museum about skiing in New Mexico, and even from this point, the view across the city is very good—you may want to come to the casual Mexican restaurant here, **Sandiago's** (38 Tramway Rd., 505/856-6692, 11 A.M.–8:30 P.M. daily, $10), for a sunset margarita (one of which, the Doogie, honors Albuquerque actor Neil Patrick Harris, who attended a nearby high school).

Petroglyph National Monument

Albuquerque's west side is bordered by this national reserve area, 7,500 acres of black boulders that crawl with some 20,000 carved lizards, birds, and assorted odd beasts. Most of the images, which were created by chipping away the blackish surface "varnish" of the volcanic rock to reach the paler stone beneath, are between 400 and 700 years old, while others may date back three millennia. A few more recent examples of rock art include Maltese crosses made by Spanish settlers and initials left by explorers (not to mention a few by idle 20th-century teenagers).

COURTESY ALBUQUERQUE CVB/@VERNA WOOD

Critters adorn the rocks at Petroglyph National Monument.

Stop in first at the **visitors center** (Unser Blvd. at Western Trail, 505/899-0205, www.nps.gov/petr, 8 A.M.–5 P.M. daily) for park maps, flyers on flora and fauna, and general orientation. You can see some of the largest groupings on two major trails: **Boca Negra Canyon,** a short paved loop, and in **Rinconada Canyon,** a 1.25-mile one-way hike. Boca Negra Canyon is the only fee area ($1/car on weekdays, $2 on weekends), and there are restrooms and water in the parking area. The Rinconada trailhead is less developed; the walk can be tedious going in some spots because the ground is sandy, but it's relatively flat. The clearest, most impressive images are in the canyon at the end of the trail. Keep an eye out for millipedes, which thrive in this stark environment; dead, their curled-up shells resemble the spirals carved on the rocks—coincidence? You can also explore in the northernmost section of the reserve, **Piedras Marcadas Canyon,** on a few trails that start in the backyards of the homes bordering the area; maps are available at the visitors center.

The back (west) side of the parkland, the **Volcanoes Day Use Area** (9 A.M.–5 P.M. daily) is also a great place to survey the city. Access is via Atrisco Vista Boulevard (exit 149) off I-40; turn right (east) 4.3 miles north of the highway at an unmarked dirt road to the parking area. From the base of three cinder cones, you can look down on the city and see how the lava flowed between sandstone bluffs that later crumbled away—hence the lava "fingers" that stretch east and the crumbled edges of the escarpment where the petroglyphs are found. If you go in the winter, you'll see that the volcanoes, which were last reported emitting steam in 1881, are still not entirely dead: Patches of green plants flourish around the steam vents that stud the hillocks, particularly visible on the middle of the three volcanoes.

Anderson-Abruzzo Albuquerque International Balloon Museum

Boosters of Albuquerque's hot air balloon scene—which has been flourishing since the first rally in 1972—include locals Ben Abruzzo, Larry Newman, and Maxie Anderson, who in 1978 made the first Atlantic crossing by balloon in the *Double Eagle II* helium craft. Abruzzo and Anderson also crossed the Pacific and set a long-distance record (5,678 miles) in the *Double Eagle V.* These pioneers are honored at The Anderson-Abruzzo Albuquerque International Balloon Museum (9201 Balloon Museum Dr. NE, 505/880-0500, www.balloonmuseum.com, 9 A.M.–5 P.M. Tues.–Sun., $4), in Balloon Fiesta Park just off East Alameda Avenue. The displays are a great mix of historical background, interactive physics lessons, and inspiring footage of record-setting balloon ventures. As long as you don't dwell too long on the zeppelin exhibit, complete with salt-and-pepper cellars from the *Hindenburg,* you'll come away inspired by the grace of balloons and wanting to take a ride in one yourself.

Los Ranchos and Corrales Scenic Byway

For a pretty drive (or bike ride) through these villages that have been all but consumed by greater Albuquerque, head north from Old Town on Rio Grande Boulevard; you first reach Los Ranchos, then cross the river at Alameda to Corrales Road and continue up the west bank. These districts remain pockets of pastoral calm where horses gambol and 18th-century acequias water organic herb gardens—a practical melding of old agricultural heritage with modern suburban bliss. The only real sights are in central Corrales, two blocks west of the main road. The folk Gothic **Old San Ysidro Church** (505/897-1513, 1–4 P.M. Sat. and Sun. June–Oct.) stands where the center of the village was in 1868, when its bulging adobe piers were first constructed.

Across the road is the village cemetery, a typically New Mexican *camposanto,* where graves are trimmed with plastic flowers and votive candles. Next door, **Casa San Ysidro** (973 Old Church Rd., 505/898-3915, www.cabq.gov/museum, $4) was owned by obsessive collectors Alan and Shirley Minge, who lived in the place from 1952 to 1997, heating with firewood and squirreling away New Mexican

© ZORA O'NEILL

Los Ranchos and Corrales are horse-friendly districts.

antiques and craftwork. The Albuquerque Museum gives tours of the interior, with its beautiful brickwork and wood carving, June–August (9:30 A.M. and 1:30 P.M. Wed.–Fri., 9:30 A.M., 10:30 A.M., and 1:30 P.M. Sat., 2 P.M. Sun.) and a little less frequently September–November and February–May (9:30 A.M. and 1:30 P.M. Wed.–Sat., 2 P.M. Sun.). You can just turn up, but it's a good idea to call to confirm the times.

Coronado State Monument

Though named for Spanish explorer Francisco Vásquez de Coronado, who camped on this lush spot by the river during his 1540 search for gold, the monument (485 Kuaua Rd., Bernalillo, 505/867-5351, 8:30 A.M.–5 P.M. Wed.–Mon., $3) is actually a Native American relic, the partially restored pueblo of Kuaua (Tiwa for "evergreen"), which was inhabited between 1300 and the early 1600s. The centerpiece is the partially sunken square kiva, its interior walls covered with murals of life-size human figures and animals in ritual poses. What you see are reproductions—the originals have been removed for preservation, and a few are on display in the visitors center. While not exactly worth its own special trip, the site is a good place to stop on your way up to Jemez, and the setting is good for a picnic. Seated on a bench facing the river and the mountains, with the city hidden from view behind a dense screen of cottonwoods, you get a sense of the lush, calm life along the Rio Grande in the centuries before the Spanish arrived. To reach the monument, exit I-25 in Bernalillo and head west on Highway 550; Kuaua Road is on your right, before the Santa Ana Star casino.

Gruet Winery

The Spanish planted the first vineyards in North America in New Mexico in the 17th century, and the industry persisted until a series of floods finally wiped out the vines by the 1920s. So New Mexico's current wine scene, while strong, is still somewhat young. One of the best wineries, Gruet (8400 Pan American Fwy. NE, 505/821-0055, www.gruetwinery.com, 10 A.M.–5 P.M. weekdays and noon–5 P.M. on Saturday) began producing its excellent sparkling wines (the Gruet family hails from Champagne) only in 1987; look out especially for its nonvintage sparkling rosé, which is delicious and affordable. The tasting room serves five pours for $6; tours of the winery run every day the room is open, at 2 P.M.

Entertainment

BARS AND CLUBS

When the city government promoted downtown as the nightlife district, it may have created too much of a good thing. Now it's the city's main bar and club scene, all packed in a few square blocks, which makes for handy hopping (or staggering) from place to place. A lot of the bars cater to students, with plentiful beer and other happy-hour specials but a somewhat generic, slightly dressed-up atmosphere. It ends in a rowdy scene after the bars close on Fridays and Saturdays and crowds spill out onto several blocks of Central that are closed to car traffic.

The more distinctive places are pure Albuquerque: unpretentious, with a remarkably varied clientele. Because there aren't enough members of any one particular subculture to pack a whole bar, even the most chic-appearing places will see an absent-minded professor and a veteran Earth Firster propping up the bar next to well-groomed professionals.

Old Town and the Rio Grande

This neighborhood doesn't offer much in the way of nightlife. The few exceptions are the rooftop patio at **Seasons** (2031 Mountain Rd. NW, 505/766-5100, 4 P.M.–11 P.M. Sun.–Thurs., 4–midnight Fri. and Sat.), where there's live jazz on weekends and happy hour Monday through Friday 4–6:30 P.M. and 9–10 P.M.

COURTESY HOTEL ANDALUZ / © SERGIO SALVADOR

Historic Hotel Andaluz was built by Conrad Hilton.

A cinder-block bunker in a random stretch of the North Valley, **Low Spirits** (2823 2nd St. NW, 505/344-9555, www.lowspiritslive.com) nonetheless is one of Albuquerque's better live-music venues, with a mix of country, indie rock, and more, all put together by the same people who run the much-admired Launchpad downtown. Cover is usually about $10, but beers can be had for $2.

Downtown

The **Hotel Andaluz lobby** (125 2nd St. NW, 505/242-9090) touts itself as "Albuquerque's living room"—Conrad Hilton's original vision for the place—and it's a comfy spot to sip delectable cocktails (the watermelon-lime cooler is dangerously drinkable) and nibble Spain-inspired snacks, especially if you reserve one of the private "casbahs" on the weekend, when there's also live tango or salsa and a big crowd of dancers. On the second floor, the indoor-outdoor **Ibiza Lounge** (from 5 P.M. Thurs.–Sat., $10 cover after 9 P.M. Fri. and Sat.) is a chic scene on weekends, a cooler alternative to

the mayhem just over on Central. Happy hour is 5–8 P.M. weekdays.

The best all-purpose casual bar downtown is the second-floor **Anodyne** (409 Central Ave. NW, 505/244-1820, 4 P.M.–1:30 A.M. Mon.–Fri., 7 P.M.–1:30 A.M. Sat., 7–11:30 P.M. Sun.), a long, wood-floor room filled with pool tables and a younger crowd sprawled on the thrift-store sofas. Choose from more than a hundred beers, and get some quarters to plug in to the good collection of pinball machines. Happy hour is 4–8 P.M. Monday to Thursday, and till 9 P.M. on Friday.

To catch the latest touring indie-rock sensation or the local crew about to hit it big, head to the very professional **Launchpad** (618 Central Ave. SW, 505/764-8887, www.launchpadrocks.com). With free live music and a pool table, **Burt's Tiki Lounge** (313 Gold Ave. SW, 505/247-2878, www.burtstikilounge.com, 8:30 P.M.–2 A.M. Mon.–Sat.) has a funky feel and an eclectic bill, from British psychedelia to reggae.

The city's best dance club is also its best

gay club: **Effex** (420 Central Ave. SW, www. effexabq.com, 9 P.M.–2 P.M. Thurs.–Sat.) is renowned for its huge dance floor and solid sound system.

Farther out of the downtown fray, the **Marble Brewery** (111 Marble Ave. NW, 505/243-2739, 1 P.M.–midnight Mon.–Sat., 1 P.M.–10:30 P.M. Sun.) is a cool space with a big patio out back, where you might catch a band: salsa, country, whatever—the crowd will dance to it, as their dogs hang out by the picnic tables. Its beers are much better than other brewpubs' in town.

The University and Nob Hill

In the Nob Hill shopping plaza, **Gecko's** (3500 Central Ave. SE, 505/262-1848, 11:30 A.M.–late Mon.–Fri., noon–late Sat. and Sun.) is a good place for a snack (anything from Thai curry shrimp to chipotle hot wings) and a drink in the sidewalk seats. Sporting its own breezy patio, **O'Niell's** (4310 Central Ave. SE, 505/255-6782, 11 A.M.–2 A.M. Mon.–Sat., 11 A.M.–midnight Sun.) is a great Irish pub

that draws a varied crowd; the kitchen is open until midnight.

If you want to watch more street life, **Kellys** (3222 Central Ave. SE, 505/262-2739, 8 A.M.–11 P.M. daily, $9) has ample outdoor seating along the sidewalk in central Nob Hill. The rich Kelly Porter washes down beer-friendly food like so-so bison burgers and curly fries—but you're really here for the scene, the sun, and the suds. If you're more in the mood for a cozy indoor vibe, head to the cellar wine bar at **Zinc** (3009 Central Ave. NE, 505/254-9462, 5 P.M.–1 A.M. Mon.–Sat., 5–11 P.M. Sun.), where you can try tasting flights while listening to a jazz trio or watching old movies.

LIVE MUSIC

Albuquerque's arts scene graces a number of excellent stages. The most beautiful of them, the city-owned **KiMo Theater** (423 Central Ave. NW, 505/768-3544, www.cabq.gov/kimo), often hosts locally written plays and dance, as well as the occasional musical performance

the Roy E. Disney Center for Performing Arts at the National Hispanic Cultural Center

CEREMONIAL DANCES

This is only an approximate schedule for ceremonial dances at Albuquerque-area pueblos – dates can vary from year to year. Annual feast days typically involve carnivals and markets in addition to dances. Confirm details and start times – usually afternoon, but sometimes following an evening or midnight Mass – with the **Indian Pueblo Cultural Center** (505/843-7270, www.indianpueblo. org) before setting out.

JANUARY 1

- Jemez: Matachines

JANUARY 6

- Most pueblos: various dances

FEBRUARY 2

- San Felipe: various dances for Candlemas (Día de la Candelaria)

EASTER

- Most pueblos: various dances

MAY 1

- San Felipe: Feast of San Felipe

JUNE 13

- Sandia: Feast of San Antonio

JUNE 29

- Santa Ana: Feast of San Pedro

JULY 14

- Cochiti: Feast of San Bonaventura

JULY 26

- Laguna: harvest dances

- Santa Ana: Feast of Santa Ana

AUGUST 2

- Jemez: Feast of Santa Persingula

AUGUST 10

- Acoma (Acomita): Feast of San Lorenzo

AUGUST 15

- Laguna (Mesita): various dances

- Zia: Feast of the Assumption of Our Blessed Mother

AUGUST 28

- Isleta: Feast of Saint Augustine

SEPTEMBER 2

- Acoma (Sky City): Feast of San Estevan

SEPTEMBER 4

- Isleta: Feast of Saint Augustine

SEPTEMBER 8

- Isleta (Encinal): Feast of the Nativity of the Blessed Virgin

SEPTEMBER 19

- Laguna (Old Laguna): Feast of Saint Joseph

SEPTEMBER 25

- Laguna (Paguate): Feast of Saint Elizabeth

OCTOBER 17

- Laguna (Paraje): Feast of Saint Margaret Mary

OCTOBER 24-27

- Laguna (Old Laguna): harvest dance

NOVEMBER 12

- Jemez: Feast of San Diego

DECEMBER 12

- Jemez: Matachines

DECEMBER 24

- Acoma (Sky City): luminaria display

- Laguna and Santa Ana: dances after midnight Mass

and film screening. Bigger acts visit the **Roy E. Disney Center for Performing Arts** at the National Hispanic Cultural Center (1701 4th St. SW, 505/724-4771, www.nhccnm.org), a modernized Mesoamerican pyramid that contains three venues, the largest of which is a 691-seat proscenium theater. This is the place to catch a performance by visiting or local flamenco artists—with the National Institute of Flamenco headquarters in Albuquerque, there's often someone performing. UNM's **Popejoy Hall** (UNM campus, 505/277-3824, www.popejoyhall.com) hosts the New Mexico Symphony Orchestra (which also plays at the Rio Grande Zoo in the summer).

Albuquerque is usually a stop for many bands' national tours. Check the schedules at the casinos, which offer not only the enticing jingle of slot machines, but also excellent stages. These relatively intimate auditoriums, with low ticket prices, are where you might catch a legend such as Merle Haggard or Etta James. The ritzier **Sandia Casino** (I-25 at Tramway, 800/526-9366, www.sandiacasino.com) has a great outdoor amphitheater and usually vies with the **Hard Rock Hotel & Casino** (11000 Broadway SE, 505/724-3800, www.hardrockcasinoabq.com), run by Isleta Pueblo, for the biggest touring names. Laguna Pueblo's **Route 66 Casino** (14500 Central Ave. SW, 866/352-7866, www.rt66casino.com) is smaller and funkier.

Also see what's on at **El Rey Theater** (620 Central Ave. SW, 505/242-2353, www.elreytheater.com) and **Sunshine Theater** (120 Central Ave. SW, 505/764-0249, www.sunshinetheaterlive.com)—both converted movie houses, they have excellent sightlines. **Outpost Performance Space** (210 Yale Blvd. SE, 505/268-0044, www.outpostspace.org) books very good world music and dance acts.

THEATER

Albuquerque has the liveliest theater scene in the Southwest, with some 30 troupes in action. You can catch local thespians at **Albuquerque Little Theater** (224 San Pasquale St. SW, 505/242-4750, www.albuquerquelittletheatre.org), founded in 1930, and the **Vortex**

(2004½ Central Ave. SE, 505/247-8600, www.vortexabq.org), near the university. The latter is Albuquerque's longest-running avant-garde space, putting up everything from Beckett to local playwrights' work in its black box since 1976. The **Filling Station** (1024 4th St. SW, www.fillingstationabq.com) hosts several local theater companies. Also check in to see what the **Tricklock Company** (www.tricklock.com) is up to—its creative productions and the international festival it hosts (in January and February) are some of the city's best.

CINEMAS

Century 14 Downtown (100 Central Ave. SW, 505/243-9555, www.cinemark.com) devotes most of its screens to blockbusters, while the latest indie and art films are shown at **The Guild** (3405 Central Ave. NE, 505/255-1848, www.guildcinema.com), a snug single screen in Nob Hill.

CREATIVE CULTURE

A young but beloved institution, Albuquerque's **Church of Beethoven** (505/234-4611, www.churchofbeethoven.org, $15) is a Sunday-morning gathering for classical-music lovers and anyone who wants "church minus the religion," as the organizers envision it. It takes place at the funky coffee house The Kosmos (1715 5th St. NW), part of a larger warehouse-turned-art-studios complex. The "service" starts at 10:30 A.M. and lasts about an hour, with two musical performances, interspersed with a poem and a few minutes of silent contemplation. It's all fueled by free espresso.

FESTIVALS AND EVENTS

The city's biggest annual event is the **Albuquerque International Balloon Fiesta** (505/821-1000, www.balloonfiesta.com), nine days in October dedicated to New Mexico's official state aircraft, with more than 700 hot air balloons of all colors, shapes, and sizes gathering at a dedicated park on the north side of town, west of I-25. During the fiesta, the city is packed with fanatical "airheads," who claim this is the best gathering of its kind in the

The annual Mariachi Spectacular gathers the best Mexican brass bands around.

world. If you go, don't miss an early-morning mass ascension, when the balloons glow against the dark sky, then lift silently into the air in a great wave. Parking can be a nightmare—take the park-and-ride bus, or ride a bike (valet parking available!).

You'll catch an equally colorful show in April at the **Gathering of Nations Powwow** (www.gatheringofnations.com), the largest tribal get-together in the United States, with more than 3,000 dancers and singers in full regalia from over 500 tribes crowding the floor of the University Arena. Miss Indian World earns her crown by showing off traditional talents such as spearfishing or storytelling.

Labor Day weekend is dedicated to the **New Mexico Wine Festival** (505/867-3311, www.newmexicowinefestival.com), which takes place in Bernalillo. It's well attended by a wide swath of Burqueños; the Rail Runner runs on a special schedule, sparing stress on designated drivers.

Just after Labor Day, the state's agricultural roots get their due at the **New Mexico State Fair** (www.exponm.com), two weeks of fried

foods and prizewinning livestock. It's your usual mix of midway craziness and exhibition barns, along with really excellent rodeos, which often end with shows by country music legends like Willie Nelson. All that Americana is countered by **Globalquerque** (www.globalquerque.com), an intense two-day world-music fest that runs in mid-September. It draws top-notch pop and traditional performers from Syria, Spain, Burkina Faso, and plenty more. Concerts take place at the National Hispanic Cultural Center.

Around November 2, don't miss the **Day of the Dead Parade** (505/363-1326, www.muertosymarigolds.org) in the South Valley, also known as the Marigold Parade, for the bright-orange flower that's associated with this Mexican festival for honoring the departed. A procession of skeletons and cars bedecked in marigolds begins by the sheriff's station on Isleta Boulevard, south of Arenal Boulevard, winds through the neighborhood, and ends with a big party at the Westside Community Center (1250 Isleta Blvd. SW).

For the holidays, the city is bedecked with

luminarias (paper-bag lanterns), especially in Old Town and the Country Club neighborhood just to the south. The Albuquerque Botanic Garden (www.abq.gov/biopark) is decked out with holiday lights and model trains for much of December, and ABQ Ride, the city bus service, offers a bus tour around the prettiest neighborhoods on Christmas Eve.

The rest of the year, look out for specialist get-togethers, such as the **National Fiery** **Foods Show** (www.fieryfoodsshow.com) in March, where capsaicin fanatics try out hot new products; the **Mariachi Spectacular** (www.mariachispectacular.com) in early July; and the weeklong **Festival Flamenco Internacional** (www.nationalinstituteofflamenco.org) in June, the largest event of its kind in the United States, with performances and workshops sponsored by the National Institute of Flamenco, which has its conservatory here.

Shopping

Albuquerque doesn't have Santa Fe's exotic treasure troves and tony galleries, but it doesn't have the high prices either. Old Town and the environs are where you can pick up traditional American Indian jewelry and pottery for very reasonable prices, while Nob Hill is the commercial center of Albuquerque's counterculture, with body-piercing studios adjacent to comic book shops next to herbal apothecaries.

On the first Friday of each month, **Artscrawl** (www.artscrawlabq.org) keeps galleries and shops open late in both neighborhoods and downtown; on the third Friday of the month, the festivities are focused in one neighborhood.

There are a number of **farmers markets** throughout the city; one of the largest is downtown at Robinson Park on Central Avenue at 8th Street (7–11 A.M. Sat. June–Oct.), and

Skip Maisel's, a classic Western-wear emporium

© ZORA O'NEILL

there's another good one in Los Ranchos (6718 Rio Grande Blvd. NW, 7–11 A.M. Sat. May–mid-Nov., 10 A.M.–noon second Sat. of the month Dec.–Apr.). For more info, see www.farmersmarketsnm.org.

OLD TOWN AND THE RIO GRANDE

The slew of galleries and gift shops packed around the plaza can blur together after just a little bit of browsing, but a couple of places stand out: **Hispaniae** (410 Romero St. NW, 505/244-1533, 10 A.M.–5:30 P.M. Mon.–Sat., noon–5 P.M. Sun.) is three rooms crammed with Mexican craftwork. The **Blue Portal Gallery** (2107 Church St. NW, 505/243-6005, 10 A.M.–4:30 P.M. Mon.–Sat., 1–4 P.M. Sun.) has well-priced and often very refined arts and crafts, from quilts to woodwork, by Albuquerque's senior citizens. And the **street vendors** set up on the east side of the plaza are all artisans selling their own work, at fair prices.

Just outside of Old Town's historic zone, the **Gertrude Zachary** showroom (1501 Lomas Blvd. NW, 505/247-4442, 9:30 A.M.–6 P.M. Mon.–Sat., 10 A.M.–5 P.M. Sun.) is the place to go for contemporary turquoise-and-silver jewelry. For more traditional work, head to the shop at the **Indian Pueblo Cultural Center** (2401 12th St. NW, 505/843-7270, www.indianpueblo.org, 9 A.M.–5 P.M. daily); not only are its prices reasonable, but the staff is happy to explain the work that goes into various pieces.

Up in Los Ranchos, **Wagon Mound Ranch Supply** (6855 4th St. NW, 505/341-2489, 9:30 A.M.–5:30 P.M. Mon.–Sat.) is an urbanized farm store, with useful stuff like Dutch ovens and enamel coffee pots, as well as Western swing music and books on knot-tying.

Even more rustic: the gorgeous **Los Poblanos Farm Shop** (4803 Rio Grande Blvd. NW, 505/938-2192, 9 A.M.–5 P.M. daily), adjacent to the lavender fields at this historic inn. The shop sells soaps, bath salts, and lotion scented with the organic lavender, as well as other seasonal creations, plus books, home items, and locally made snacks. Say hi to the goats in the barn next door!

Even farther north, along 4th Street between Montaño and Ortega in Los Ranchos, is a strip of shops collectively called the **Antique Mile.** There are about a dozen huge stores and converted houses crammed with jewelry, vintage clothing, furniture, and architectural salvage.

DOWNTOWN

Sears Roebuck and JCPenney have moved on, but a few interesting shops still occupy the curved show windows along Central. An emporium of American Indian goods, **Skip Maisel's Indian Jewelry & Crafts** (510 Central Ave. SW, 505/242-6526, 9 A.M.–5:30 P.M. Mon.–Sat.) feels like a relic from downtown's heyday—whether you want a war bonnet, a turquoise-studded watch, or deerskin moccasins, it's all here in a vast, overstocked shop with kindly salespeople. Don't miss the beautiful murals above the display windows and in the foyer; they were painted in the 1930s by local Indian artists such as Awa Tsireh, whose work hangs in the New Mexico Museum of Art in Santa Fe. Another throwback is **The Man's Hat Shop** (511 Central Ave. NW, 505/247-9605, 9:30 A.M.–5:30 P.M. Tues.–Fri., 9:30 A.M.–5 P.M. Sat.), which stocks just what it promises, from homburgs to ten-gallons.

THE UNIVERSITY AND NOB HILL

Start your stroll on the west end of the Nob Hill district, near Girard. **Masks y Más** (3106 Central Ave. SE, 505/256-4183, 11 A.M.–6 P.M. Mon.–Thurs., 11 A.M.–7 P.M. Fri., noon–5 P.M. Sun.) deals in all things bizarre, most with a south-of-the-border flavor; here's where to get the outfit for your Mexican-wrestler alter ego. A few blocks down, tasteful **Hey Jhonny** (3418 Central Ave. SE, 505/256-9244, 10 A.M.–6:30 P.M. Mon.–Sat., 11 A.M.–6 P.M. Sun.) stocks gorgeous sushi sets, hip handbags, and travel guides only to the coolest destinations.

On the next corner, **Mariposa Gallery** (3500 Central Ave. SE, 505/268-6828, 11 A.M.–6 P.M. Mon.–Sat., noon–5 P.M. Sun.) is one of the city's longest-established art vendors, dealing since 1974 in jewelry, fiber art, and other crafts. If you're looking for unusual postcards, head down the block to **Papers!** (108 Amherst Dr. SE, 505/254-1434, 10:30 A.M.–6:30 P.M. Mon.–Sat., 11 A.M.–5 P.M. Sun.), where the greeting cards are great but the array of blank sheets may inspire you to make your own. **The A Store** (3500 Central Ave. SE, 505/266-2222, 10 A.M.–6 P.M. Mon.–Sat., noon–5 P.M. Sun.) specializes in home furnishings for the Southwestern hipster, such as colorful flower-print Mexican tablecloth fabric and hand-made candles. The jewelry here, much of it by local designers, is very good, too.

Nob Hill's hip businesses expand a little farther east every year—now "upper Nob Hill" extends east of Carlisle, and you can keep strolling this way for highlights such as the **Absolutely Neon** gallery of new and vintage signs (3903 Central Ave. NE, 505/265-6366, 11 A.M.–6 P.M. Mon.–Sat.) and, farther on, a whole slew of antiques marts, comparable to those in Los Ranchos.

ALBUQUERQUE METRO AREA

Every Saturday and Sunday, Albuquerque's **flea market** (505/222-9766, $5 parking) takes place at the fairgrounds (enter at Gate 9, on Louisiana just north of Central). It's an interesting outlet where you can pick up anything from new cowboy boots to loose nuggets of turquoise; socks and beef jerky are also well represented. Stop off at one of the myriad food stands for a snack—refreshing *aguas frescas* (fruit juices, in flavors such as watermelon and tamarind) and Indian frybread are the most popular. It allegedly starts at 7 A.M., but most vendors get rolling around 9 A.M. and go till a little after 4 P.M.

Sports and Recreation

Albuquerque is a perfect city for outdoorsy types, with several distinct ecosystems and trails running through all of them. Late spring and summer are the best times to head to the higher elevations on the Sandia Mountains. Once the cool fall weather sets in, the scrub-covered foot-hills and the bare, rocky West Mesa are more hospitable. The valley along the Rio Grande, running through the center of the city, is remarkably pleasant year-round: mild in winter and cool and shady in summer. As everywhere in the desert, always pack extra layers of clothing and plenty of water before you set out, and don't go charging up Sandia Peak (10,678 feet above sea level) your first day off the plane.

BALLOONING

You don't have to be in town for the Balloon Fiesta to go up, up, and away: Take a morning hot-air balloon ride with **Rainbow Ryders** (505/823-1111, www.rainbowryders.com, $150 per person) to get a true bird's-eye view of the city. Typically, you're up in the balloon for an hour or so, depending on wind conditions, and you get a champagne toast when you're back on solid ground.

SKIING

Sandia Peak Ski Area (505/242-9052, www.sandiapeak.com, $50 full-day lift ticket) is open from mid-December through mid-March, though it often takes till about February for a good base to build up. The 30 trails, serviced by four lifts, are not dramatic, but they are good and long. The area is open daily in the holiday season, then Wednesday through Sunday for the rest of the winter.

Sandia Peak also has plenty of opportunities for cross-country skiing. Groomed trails head out from **Capulin Springs Snowplay Area,** where there are also big hills for tubing and sledding (9:30 A.M.–3:30 P.M. Fri.–Sun. in winter, $3/car). Look for the parking nine miles up Highway 536 to the crest. Farther up on the mountain, **10K Trail** is usually groomed for skiers, as is a service road heading south to

Albuquerque's landscape offers various options for outdoor recreation.

the upper tramway terminal; the latter is wide and relatively level—good for beginners. You can check the status of the trails at the Sandia ranger station (505/281-3304) on Highway 337 in Tijeras.

HIKING

Between the West Mesa and the east mountains, Albuquerque offers a huge range of day hikes. The least strenuous option is the *bosque* (the wooded area along the Rio Grande), where level paths lead through groves of cottonwoods, willows, and olive trees. The **Rio Grande Nature Center** (8 A.M.–5 P.M. daily, $3/car), at the end of Candelaria, is the best starting point for any walk around the area. The **Los Poblanos Fields Open Space** is also a great non-strenuous outdoor area—really, it's 138 acres of farmland that the city owns in the North Valley. Part of the land is given over to grain cultivation to attract migrating birds. Trails loop through the fields and along the irrigation ditches, and there's a corn maze in fall, as well as regular weekend activities.

Anyone looking for some elevation gain will want to head to the Sandias. On the city side, the foothills are ideal in the winter but a little hot in the summertime—the best access is at **Elena Gallegos Picnic Area** (7 A.M.–9 P.M. Apr.–Oct., 7 A.M.–7 P.M. Nov.–Mar., $1 weekdays, $2 weekends), east of Tramway Boulevard and north of Academy, at the end of Simms Park Road.

The foothills are also the starting point for a much more challenging hike: the popular **La Luz Trail,** a 7.5-mile ascent to the Sandia Crest Visitor Center. The trail has a 12 percent grade at certain points, but the views are worth the effort, as is the experience of hiking through four climate zones (pack lots of layers) as you climb 3,200 vertical feet. The trail is perhaps the best known in the Sandias, so it's well worn; the only potentially confusing part is after about two miles, where the trail crosses a streambed and makes a sharp turn south. Near the top, you can take a spur that leads north to the Sandia Crest observation point or continue on the main trail south to the ski area and the

Sandia Peak Tramway, which you can take you back down the mountain. Ideally you'd have someone pick you up at the bottom end of the tram, because the 2.5-mile trail along the foothills from the tram back to the trailhead is dusty and lacking in shade. (You might be tempted to take the tram up and hike down, but the steep descent can be deadly to toes and knees.) La Luz trailhead ($3/car) is at the far north end of Tramway Boulevard just before the road turns west.

If you want to enjoy the views without quite so much effort, you can drive up the east face of the mountain (I-40 to Highway 14) via scenic byway Highway 536, a.k.a. the Crest Road, and park at the Sandia Crest Visitor Center at the top ($3/car). From there, an easy loop of a little more than two miles runs south along the **Crest Spur Trail,** which dips below the ridgeline to connect to **La Luz,** which in turn goes on to the tram terminal. Then you can hike back to your car via the **Crest Trail.** This is the single-most-traveled stretch on Sandia Peak; if you want to avoid the crowds, start on some of the trails lower down the mountain—**Tree Spring Trail,** in particular, five miles up the mountain, heads up to the crest and is also a convenient link to other trails. See the invaluable website Sandia Mountain Hiking Guide (www.sandiahiking.com) for more details on this and other trails, plus printable maps of the more than 180 miles of hiking available in the mountains—or pick up the book version.

BIKING

Albuquerque maintains a great network of paved trails for cycling in the city, and the mountains and foothills are lined with challenging dirt tracks.

City Cycling

Recreational cyclists need head no farther than the river, where the **Paseo del Bosque,** a 16-mile-long, completely flat biking and jogging path, runs through the Rio Grande Valley State Park. The natural starting point is at **Alameda/Rio Grande Open Space** (7 A.M.–9 P.M. daily Apr.–Oct., 7 A.M.–7 P.M.

daily Nov.–Mar.) on Alameda Boulevard. You can also reach the trail through the **Rio Grande Nature Center** (8 A.M.–5 P.M. daily, $3/car), at the end of Candelaria, and at several other major intersections along the way. For details on this and other bike trails in Albuquerque, download a map from the city's bike info page (www.cabq.gov/bike), or pick up a free copy at bike shops around town. In the summer, you can **rent bikes** at Tingley Beach (part of the Albuquerque BioPark, in the *Sights* section; 10 A.M.–5 P.M. Mon.–Fri., 10 A.M.–6 P.M. Sat. and Sun., $8/hour, $20/4 hours) and start biking along the river from there. **Routes** (1102 Mountain Rd. NW, 505/933-5667, 9 A.M.–6 P.M. daily Apr.–Nov., 10 A.M.–5 P.M. daily Dec.–Mar., $15/hour, $35/day) does year-round rentals and has a handy location between Old Town and downtown; it also rents snowshoes in the winter.

Corrales is also good for an afternoon bike ride: The speed limit on the main street is low, and you can dip into smaller side streets and bike along the acequias. The excellent **Stevie's Happy Bikes** (4583 Corrales Rd., 505/897-7900, 10 A.M.–6 P.M. Tues.–Sat.) rents comfy cruisers ($25/day) and even tandems ($35/day) and can advise on the best routes on and around the river. You could bike along the road one direction, perhaps stopping at the church and Casa San Ysidro, and then loop back on the riverfront path, an extension of the Paseo del Bosque. In about four hours, you can make a leisurely loop down to Los Poblanos farms and open space and get back up to Corrales.

Mountain Biking

Mountain bikers can take the Sandia Peak Tramway to the ski area, then rent wheels to explore the 30 miles of wooded trails. Bikes aren't allowed on the tram, though, so if you have your own ride, you can drive around the east side of the mountain. Advanced riders will appreciate the challenge of rocky **Faulty Trail,** which runs about 11 miles north–south along the lower elevations of Sandia Peak, connecting with other trails that lead down to main roads as well as higher up the mountain. One access point, midway along the route, is from Highway 14: Coming from I-40, turn left after 3.4 miles onto Cañoncito Road (*not* Corte de Cañoncito); stay on this main road for half a mile, bearing right at a fork partway along; just as the paving ends, bear left onto Cole Springs Road and then park at the pullout here. Continue up to the road, past some fencing, to a locked gate; the next mile of road is private property (which you may cross on foot), and then you reach the Cañoncito trailhead. This trail leads up 0.75 mile to the intersection with Faulty, just after Cañoncito Spring—the more challenging sections are to the north, or right (heading left brings you into the Sandia Mountain Wilderness, where mountain biking is prohibited). You can also get access to the trail near its north end, via the Sulphur Canyon Trail, which leads out of Doc Long Picnic Ground, about 2 miles up the Crest Road.

Or you can stay in the city and explore the foothills. Locals built the small but fun **Embudo Mountain Bike Terrain Park** at the end of Indian School Road; it is packed with jumps and berms. For a longer cruise, head for the **foothills trails,** a web of dirt tracks all along the edge of the Northeast Heights. **Trail no. 365,** which runs for about 15 miles north–south from near the tramway down to near I-40, is the best run. You can start at either end, or go to the midpoint, at Elena Gallegos Open Space, off the north end of Tramway Boulevard at the end of Simms Park Road. Elena Gallegos in particular is very popular, so go on a weekday if you can, and always look out for hikers and other bikers. Aside from the occasional sandy or rocky patch, none of the route is technical or steep. More complex trails run off to the east; pick up a map at the entrance booth at Elena Gallegos.

Road Biking

For hard-core road bikers, a popular tour is up to **Sandia Peak** via the Crest Road on the east side—you can park and ride from any point, but cyclists typically start somewhere along Highway 14 (the Turquoise Trail) north of I-40, then ride up Highway 536, which winds 13.5 miles along increasingly steep switchbacks to the crest. The New Mexico Touring Society (www.nmts.org) lists descriptions of the myriad of other ride options and organizes group rides.

SPECTATOR SPORTS

Minor-league baseball thrives in Albuquerque, apparently all because of some clever name: The so-so Dukes petered out a while back, but a fresh franchise, under the name of the **Albuquerque Isotopes,** has been drawing crowds since 2003. It's hard to judge whether the appeal is the cool Isotopes Park (1601 Avenida Cesar Chavez NE, 505/924-2255, www.albuquerquebaseball.com), the whoopee-cushion theme nights, or just the name, drawn from an episode of *The Simpsons*. Regardless, a summer night under the ballpark lights is undeniably pleasant; it helps that you can usually get good seats for $15.

For an even smaller-scale ball game, you can head up to the ball field at Santa Ana pueblo

Root for the home team at Isotopes Park.

(near Bernalillo), home of the Tamaya Tigers, where semipro pueblo teams, as well as Navajo teams from Shiprock and Gallup, face off all summer long. (Isotopes Park then hosts the All-Indian All-Star Playoffs when the pueblo tournament season wraps up in mid-September.)

Albuquerqueans also go crazy for UNM Lobos **basketball,** packing the raucous University Arena, a.k.a. "The Pit" (Avenida Cesar Chavez at University Blvd., 505/925-5626, www.golobos.com).

SPAS AND SPORTS FACILITIES

Betty's Bath & Day Spa (1835 Candelaria Rd. NW, 505/341-3456, www.bettysbath.com) is the place to get pampered, whether with a massage and a facial or with an extended dip in one of two outdoor communal hot tubs. One is co-ed and the other for women only; both have access to dry saunas and cold plunges—a bargain at just $12. Private reservations are available most evenings. Closer to downtown, **Albuquerque Baths** (1218 Broadway NE, 505/505/243-3721, www.abqbaths.com) has similar facilities, though only one communal tub that's solar-heated; the sauna is done in Finnish cedar. The reasonable rates ($15, or $10 before 3 P.M.) include the use of robes and sandals, and massages are available too.

Beat the heat at the **Rio Grande Pool** (1410 Iron Ave. SW, 505/848-1397, noon–5 P.M. daily, $2.25), one of Albuquerque's nicest places to take a dip; the outdoor 25-meter pool is shaded by giant cottonwoods.

Accommodations

Because Albuquerque isn't quite a tourist mecca, its hotel offerings have languished a bit, but the scene has improved in recent years. There are still plenty of grungy places, but the good ones are exceptional values. Whether on the low or high end, you'll pay substantially less here than you would in Santa Fe for similar amenities.

UNDER $100

Funky and affordable, the **Route 66 Hostel** (1012 Central Ave. SW, 505/247-1813, www.rt66hostel.com) is in a century-old house midway between downtown and Old Town and has been offering bargain accommodations since 1978; it's clean despite years of budget travelers traipsing through. Upstairs, along creaky wood hallways, are private rooms ($25–35) with various configurations. Downstairs and in the cool basement area are single-sex dorms ($20 pp). Guests have run of the kitchen, and there's a laundry and room to lounge. The most useful city bus lines run right out front. There have been complaints of staff not being on hand for early or late check-ins—be sure to call and confirm before you arrive.

If you're on a budget but have your own car, you can also stay on the east side of the Sandias, about a half-hour drive from the city. The **Cedar Crest Inn** (12231 Hwy. 14, 505/281-4117) is peaceful, with an orchard out back, and very inexpensive lodging, including a dorm option ($20 pp). The dorm area is very well kept, though it's screened from the big shared kitchen only by a curtain. Upstairs are three private rooms ($50–75). Just up the road on the west side, the **Turquoise Trail Campground** (22 Calvary Rd., 505/281-2005, May–Oct.) has tree-shaded spots for tents ($17.50) as well as two small cabins ($36; no water) and one large one with a bathroom and kitchenette, along with showers and laundry facilities.

The only criticism to muster against the **Sandia Peak Inn** (4614 Central Ave. SW, 505/831-5036, $60 d) is that it's nowhere near the mountain; in fact, it's on the west side of the city, just over the river from Old Town. In all other respects, it's more than you could want in a bargain hotel: large, spotless rooms, all with bathtubs, fridges, microwaves, and huge TVs. Breakfast is included in the rate. There's a small indoor pool and free wireless Internet available throughout.

Central Avenue is strewn with motels, many built in Route 66's heyday. Almost all of them are unsavory, except for ◖ **Monterey Non-Smokers Motel** (2402 Central Ave. SW, 505/243-3554, www.nonsmokersmotel.com, $64 s, $68 d), which is as practical as its name implies. Except for a jazzy neon sign, the place doesn't really capitalize on 1950s kitsch—it just offers meticulously clean, good-value rooms with no extra frills or flair. One large family suite has two beds and a foldout sofa. The pool is a treat, the laundry facilities are a bonus, and the location near Old Town is very convenient.

The Hotel Blue (717 Central Ave. NW, 877/878-4868, www.thehotelblue.com, $62 s, $72 d) offers great value downtown. The rooms in this '60s block are a slightly odd mix of cheesy motel decor (gold quilted bedspreads) and bachelor-pad flair (a gas "fireplace"), and the windows don't open. But the Tempur-Pedic beds are undeniably comfortable, and the low rates include breakfast, parking, and a shuttle to the airport. There's also a decent-size outdoor pool, open in summers, and the downtown farmers market is in the park right out front. Request a room on the northeast side for a mountain view.

$100-150

On the west edge of downtown you'll find the Queen Anne–style **Mauger Estate** (701 Roma Ave., 505/242-8755, www.maugerbb.com, $109 s). It gleams with polished dark wood paneling and floors. Luxe touches like triple-sheeted beds and fresh flowers contribute to an overall feeling of elegance.

The exceptionally tasteful ◖ **Downtown Historic Bed & Breakfasts of Albuquerque** (207 High St. NE, 505/842-0223, www.albuquerquebedandbreakfasts.com, $129 d) occupies two neighboring old houses on the east side of downtown, walking distance to good restaurants on Central in the EDo stretch. Heritage House has more of a Victorian feel,

Historic Hotel Andaluz was given a top-to-bottom makeover in 2009.

while the bungalow called Spy House has a sparer, 1940s look (and got its name because it's where David Greenberg, brother of Ethel Rosenberg, lived while he was collecting atomic secrets from Los Alamos). There are also two separate small rental houses, with kitchens—though rates still include breakfast.

The heart of **Cinnamon Morning** (2700 Rio Grande Blvd. NW, 505/345-3541, www.cinnamonmorning.com, $129 s), about a mile north of Old Town, is its lavish outdoor kitchen, with a huge round dining table and a fireplace to encourage lounging on nippier nights. Rooms are simply furnished, with minimalist Southwestern detail—choose from three smaller rooms in the main house, each with a private bath, or, across the garden, a two-bedroom guest house and a casita with a private patio and a kitchenette.

Hidden on a narrow road in the rural-feeling Los Ranchos district, **Casita Chamisa** (850 Chamisal Rd. NW, 505/897-4644, www.casitachamisa.com, $105 d) is very informal, and even a little bit worn, but really feels like staying at a friend's house (a friend who happens to have a swimming pool and an orchard). The rambling 150-year-old adobe compound is the sort of place that could exist only in New Mexico: It sits on an old acequia, amid the remnants of a Pueblo community established seven centuries ago. The site was partially excavated by the owner's late wife, an archaeologist.

Another strong option in Los Ranchos, **Sarabande B&B** (5637 Rio Grande Blvd. NW, 505/345-4923, www.sarabandebnb.com, $109 s), has six rooms in three configurations. Choose from a skylight, brick floors, and a potbellied wood stove; a private garden and a gas fireplace; or a wood-burning kiva fireplace and a soaking tub. They're all done in subdued Southwestern style. A small lap pool takes up the backyard, and a flower-filled patio with a fountain is the breakfast venue.

Nativo Lodge (6000 Pan American Fwy., 505/798-4300, www.hhandr.com, $135 d) is comparable to sister property Hotel Albuquerque in style and comfort, with

plush pillow-top beds and a cool "Pueblo Modern" style. But because it's on the north side of town—convenient only for the Balloon Fiesta or an early start to Santa Fe—it's substantially cheaper. Definitely request a room in the back, so you're not overlooking I-25, and try to book online, where the rates can drop substantially.

$150-250

A beautiful relic of early 20th-century travel, **◖ Hotel Andaluz** (125 2nd St. NW, 505/242-9090, www.hotelandaluz.com, $189 d) first opened in 1939 by New Mexico–raised hotelier Conrad Hilton. It received a massive renovation in 2009, keeping all the old wood and murals but updating the core to be fully environmentally friendly, from solar hot-water heaters to a composting program. The neutral-palette rooms are soothing and well designed, with a little Moorish flair in the curvy door outlines. The place is worth a visit for the lobby alone; check out the exhibits from local museums on the second-floor mezzanine.

Set in the original AT&SF railroad hospital and sporting a storied past, the stylishly renovated **Parq Central** (806 Central Ave. SE, 505/242-0040, www.hotelparqcentral.com, $160 s, $180 d), opened in late 2010, is a nice alternative to the Andaluz if you prefer your history in paler shades. The rooms are bit smaller but feel light and airy thanks to big windows and gray and white furnishings, with retro chrome fixtures and honeycomb tiles in the bath. The hospital vibe is largely eradicated, though whimsical vitrines in the halls conjure patent medicine, and the rooftop bar sports a gurney. Perks include free parking, decent continental breakfast, and airport shuttle.

At Albuquerque's nicest place to stay, you don't actually feel like you're anywhere near the city. **◖ Los Poblanos Historic Inn** (4803 Rio Grande Blvd. NW, 505/344-9297, www.lospoblanos.com, $175 s, $195 d) sits on 25 acres, the largest remaining plot of land in the city, and the rooms are tucked in various corners of a sprawling *rancho* built

Los Poblanos Historic Inn was built by noted architect John Gaw Meem.

in the 1930s by John Gaw Meem and beautifully maintained and preserved—even the huge old kitchen ranges are still in place, as are murals by Taos artist Gustave Baumann and frescoes by Peter Hurd. Main-house guest rooms, accented with Spanish colonial antiques and arrayed around a central patio, retain their old wood floors and heavy viga ceilings. Newer, larger rooms have been added and fit in flawlessly—Meem rooms have a very light Southwest touch, while the Farm rooms have a whitewashed rustic aesthetic, accented by prints and fabrics by modernist designer Alexander Girard, of the folk-art museum in Santa Fe. There's also a saltwater pool and a gym, but the most special feature is access to the extensive gardens and organic lavender farm that take up much of the acreage. Included breakfast is exceptional (you get eggs from the farm), as are optional light dinners—make sure you plan on at least one.

Hotel Albuquerque at Old Town (800 Rio Grande Blvd. NW, 505/843-6300, www.

hhandr.com, $169 d) is a good backup in this category—on the surface a little pricey, though rates are much lower when booked online. Sporting a chic Spanish colonial style, the brick-red-and-beige rooms are relatively spacious. Opt for the north side (generally, even-numbered rooms) for a view of the mountains.

OVER $250

The smell of piñon smoke and the sound of flute music set the tone at the **Hyatt Regency Tamaya** (1300 Tuyuna Tr., Santa Ana Pueblo, 505/867-1234, www.hyattregencytamaya. com, $265 d), an impeccably designed resort that's a cooperative project between Santa Ana Pueblo and the Hyatt chain. Even the standard rooms are quite large, with either terraces or balconies, though the mountain view is worth the premium. Three swimming pools and a full spa offer relaxation; the more active can play golf or tennis, take an archery class, or attend an evening storytelling program with a pueblo member.

Food

Although Albuquerque has a few dress-up establishments, the real spirit of the city's cuisine is in its lower-rent spots where dedicated owners follow their individual visions—whether that means funky lunch creations or the hottest chile in the state. A lot of the most traditional New Mexican places are open only for breakfast and lunch, so plan accordingly.

OLD TOWN AND THE RIO GRANDE

Aside from the couple recommended here, the restaurants in the blocks immediately adjacent to the Old Town plaza are expensive and only so-so; better to walk another block or two for real New Mexican flavor, which can be found in a number of local hangouts around Old Town and up Rio Grande Boulevard in the North Valley.

Cafés

Inside the Albuquerque Museum, **Slate Street Café** (2000 Mountain Rd. NW, 505/243-2220, 10 A.M.–3 P.M., snacks till 4 P.M. Tues.–Sun., $8) is great for coffee and cupcakes, as well as more substantial breakfast and lunch, like a chipotle-spiked meatloaf sandwich. Tucked in a courtyard on the back side of the museum, the venerable **La Crêpe Michel** (400 San Felipe St. NW, 505/242-1251, 11:30 A.M.–2 P.M. and 6–9 P.M. Tues.–Sat., $10) is unreconstructed French, from quiche Lorraine to *croques monsieurs*—in a snug front room and a covered back patio.

A 10-minute walk from Old Town, **Golden Crown Panaderia** (1103 Mountain Rd. NW, 505/243-2424, 7 A.M.–8 P.M. Tues.–Sat., 10 A.M.–8 P.M. Sun., $4–9) is a real neighborhood hangout that's so much more than a bakery. Famous for its green-chile bread and biscochitos (the anise-laced state cookie), it also does pizza with blue-corn or green-chile crust, to take away or to eat at the picnic tables out back. And you'll want a side salad just to watch them assemble it straight from the hydroponic garden that consumes a lot of the space behind the counter. Wash it down with a coffee milkshake.

On a barren stretch of North 4th Street, where neighboring businesses are feed stores and car washes, three exceptional restaurants are run by the same family. For breakfast and lunch, **C Sophia's Place** (6313 4th St. NW, 505/345-3935, 7 A.M.–3 P.M. Mon.–Fri., 9 A.M.–2 P.M. Sat. and Sun., $9) is the sort of bohemian café that serves fresh farm

BREAKING BAD: A STAR IS BORN

The AMC show about a high school chemistry teacher turned meth cook, *Breaking Bad* was originally written for a California setting, but production moved to Albuquerque following tax incentives. It was a happy accident that the producers have reveled in, and unlike other productions shot here anonymously, *Breaking Bad* is explicitly down with the 505.

Despite all the gunshots, psychotic meth dealers, and gritty details, the show displays an affection for Albuquerque that the city has rarely gotten from Hollywood. The location scouts have capitalized on urban icons such as the Dog House, a hot-dog stand at 1216 Central Avenue Southwest, near Old Town, that sports an exceptionally fine neon sign. Los Pollos Hermanos is actually Twisters, at 4257 Isleta Boulevard Southwest, but the PH logo is painted on the wall outside. The Crossroads Motel, where Wendy lives and turns tricks, is on Central by I-25. And the car wash that Walt works in and buys is at Menaul and Eubank.

If you're into the show, or just generally curious about the movie scene in Albuquerque, be sure to take the ABQ Trolley tour (see *Sights*), which passes many filming locations and the studios by the rail yard.

eggs but doesn't brag about it. Get those eggs on a breakfast sandwich, which you're really ordering for the side of highly addictive red-chile-dusted home fries. For dinner, head to **Ezra's Place** (6132 4th St. NW, 505/344-1917, 5–9 p.m. Tues.–Fri., 9 a.m.–2 p.m. and 5–9 p.m. Sat., 9 a.m.–2 p.m. Sun., $13), which has a similarly eclectic menu with tons of specials every day, inspired by whatever's in season. A major selling point, on top of dishes like duck enchiladas with serrano-tomatillo salsa, is the location in a bowling alley (look for the sign for Lucky 66 Lanes). And if you're just craving a burger, get one at **Jo's Place** (6100-B 4th St. NW, 505/341-4500, 8 a.m.–4 p.m. daily, $10), where they're towering and succulent; lighter eaters will like the super-chickeny tortilla soup.

New Mexican

Don't waste your time on restaurants around the plaza. Instead, walk a couple of blocks to **Duran Central Pharmacy** (1815 Central Ave. NW, 505/247-4141, 9 a.m.–6:30 p.m. Mon.–Fri., 9 a.m.–2 p.m. Sat., $9), an old-fashioned lunch counter hidden behind the magazine rack in this big fluorescent-lit drugstore. Regulars pack this place at lunch for all the New Mexican staples: huevos rancheros, green-chile stew, and big enchilada plates. Cash only.

For New Mexican food with a heavier American Indian influence, hit the **Pueblo Harvest Café** (2401 12th St. NW, 505/724-3510, 8 a.m.–8:30 p.m. Mon.–Thurs., 8 a.m.–9 p.m. Fri. and Sat., 8 a.m.–4 p.m. Sun., $10), at the Indian Pueblo Cultural Center. The menu has standard burgers and fries, but specialties such as mutton stew with a side of *horno* bread and a green-chile-and-lamb sandwich are rich and earthy and rarely found elsewhere. Breakfast is also good, with blue-corn pancakes and apple-raisin "Indian toast." The "Rez Breakfast," with Spam on the side, may be a treat for some. There's live music Friday and Saturday evenings, as well as Sunday around noon.

Mexican

The facade of **Ranch Market** (4201 Central

Beyond these doors lies Mexico.

Ave. NW, 505/833-1765, 7 A.M.–11 P.M. daily, $5) hardly hints at the wonders inside. If you haven't been in one of these (they're an Arizona-based chain), step inside for a bonus travel experience, straight to Mexico. The big-box-y shelves are lined with Bimbo bread and other south-of-the-border essentials, but the real action is in the food court, past the cash registers and to the left, where's a dazzling array of quesadillas, *sincronizadas,* tamales, and more, with a separate station for fresh fruit juices.

DOWNTOWN

With so many bars in this area, there's little room left for food, beyond a couple of solid cafés.

Cafés

A branch of **Flying Star** (723 Silver Ave. SE, 505/244-8099, 6 A.M.–10 P.M. Sun.–Thurs., 6 A.M.–11 P.M. Fri. and Sat., $10) occupies a hiply restored 1950 John Gaw Meem bank building. See *The University and Nob Hill* listings for more.

Past the railroad tracks in EDo (East Downtown), **《 The Grove** (600 Central Ave. SE, 505/248-9800, 7 A.M.–4 P.M. Tues.–Sat., 8 A.M.–3 P.M. Sun., $10) complements its local-organic menu with an indoor-outdoor feel, with big front windows facing Central and a screened-in patio. The chalkboard menu features big, creative salads (spinach, orange slices, and dates is one combo) as well as sandwiches and cupcakes; breakfast, with farm-fresh local eggs and homemade English muffins, is served all day. It's a notch above Flying Star in price, but you're paying for the especially high-quality ingredients.

The Grove's funkier neighbor, **The Daily Grind** (414 Central Ave. SE, 505/883-8310, 7 A.M.–4 P.M. Mon.–Fri., 7:30 A.M.–4 P.M. Sat., 9 A.M.–3 P.M. Sun., $8) is wedged in one of the last remaining old adobes in the area, with a patio out back. Lunch specials change every day, ranging from green-chile quiche to crab cakes.

New Mexican

Even though it's in the middle of Albuquerque's main business district, **Cecilia's Café** (230 6th

Cecilia's Café is a bit of home style amid the downtown office buildings.

© ZORA O'NEILL

St. SW, 505/243-7070, 7 A.M.–3 P.M. daily, $8) feels more like a living room than an office. Maybe it's the woodstove in the corner—as well as the personal attention from Cecilia and her daughters and the food that's clearly made with care. The rich, dark red chile really shines here.

Pizza

A popular hangout with urban pioneers in the EDo neighborhood, **Farina Pizzeria** (510 Central Ave. SE, 505/243-0130, 11 A.M.–9 P.M. Mon., 11 A.M.–10 P.M. Tues.–Fri., 4–10 P.M. Sat., 5–9 P.M. Sun., $13) has exposed brick walls and a casual vibe. The pies come out of the wood-fired oven suitably crisp-chewy and topped with seasonal veggies—make sure you get a cup of the gorgonzola-crème fraiche-chive dip for your crusts. There's usually a pasta special as well.

If you're on the go—or just prefer to soak up the sun on the 4th Street pedestrian walk—you can grab a slice at **JC's New York Pizza Department** (215 Central Ave. NW, 505/766-6973, 11 A.M.–midnight Sun.–Thurs., 11 A.M.–2:30 A.M. Fri. and Sat., $6), which specializes in thin-crust pies named after the five boroughs (Da Bronx: pepperoni and mozzarella).

THE UNIVERSITY AND NOB HILL

Thanks to the large student population, this area has some great and varied spots to grab a cheap bite, but Nob Hill has some upscale options too.

Cafés

When you walk into **◖ Flying Star** (3416 Central Ave. SE, 505/255-6633, 6 A.M.–11:30 P.M. Mon.–Thurs., 6 A.M.–midnight Fri. and Sat., $10), you'll be mesmerized by the pastry case, packed with triple-ginger cookies, lemon-blueberry cheesecake, and fat éclairs. But try to look up to appreciate the range on the menu boards: Asian noodles, hot and cold sandwiches, mac-and-cheese, and enchiladas. The food isn't always quite as great as it looks, but with speedy service and

locations all over town, it's a handy place to zip in or to lounge around (wireless Internet access is free). You'll find one in nearly every neighborhood, including the North Valley (4026 Rio Grande Blvd. NW, 505/344-6714) and downtown.

Just a few blocks from the university, **Annapurna World Vegetarian Café** (2201 Silver Ave. SE, 505/262-2424, 9 A.M.–9 P.M. Mon.–Sat., 10 A.M.–8 P.M. Sun., $9) is a vegetarian's delight, serving a menu that's compatible with Ayurvedic dietary recommendations, with giant masala dosas (rice-flour crepes) as well as less strictly Indian dishes such as cardamom pancakes with maple syrup. It has a second branch in the North Valley (7520 4th St. NW, 505/254-2424, 9 A.M.–9 P.M. Mon.–Sat.).

Pick up goods for a picnic at **La Montañita Co-op** (3500 Central Ave. SE, 505/265-4631, 7 A.M.–10 P.M. Mon.–Sat., 8 A.M.–10 P.M. Sun.), where quinoa salads and stuffed grape leaves are all the rage; look in the dairy section for "sampler" pieces of locally made cheese. There's a snacks-only operation in the UNM Bookstore, across from the Frontier (2301 Central Ave. NE, 505/277-9586, 7 A.M.–6 P.M. Mon.–Fri., 10 A.M.–4 P.M. Sat.), and a bigger branch in the **North Valley** (2400 Rio Grande Blvd. NW, 505/242-8800, 7 A.M.–10 P.M. daily).

Italian

Il Vicino (3403 Central Ave. NE, 505/266-7855, 11 A.M.–11 P.M. Sun.–Thurs., 11 A.M.–midnight Fri. and Sat., $12) is a slick brewpub and pizza parlor. Order at the front counter from the list of high-grade pizza toppings, and the dough promptly gets slid into the wood-fired oven at the back—or opt for a grilled sandwich or a big fresh salad. Then squeeze into your seat and enjoy your pint of Wet Mountain IPA. In keeping with the upscale pizza-joint feel, there's also wine and Italian sodas.

For a slightly swankier Italian meal, head to **Vivace** (3118 Central Ave. SE, 505/268-5965, 11 A.M.–9 P.M. Mon.–Thurs., 11 A.M.–10 P.M. Fri. and Sat., 5–9 P.M. Sun., $16) for garlicky linguine with clams or just a nicer-than-usual plate of spaghetti and meatballs, with a good selection of Italian wines. The calm, white-tablecloth storefront dining room makes a nice break from enchiladas and greasy spoons.

New Mexican

You haven't been to Albuquerque unless you've been to **The Frontier** (2400 Central Ave. SE, 505/266-0550, 5 A.M.–1 A.M. daily, $6), across from UNM. Everyone in the city passes through its doors at some point in their lives, so all you have to do is pick a seat in one of the five Western-theme rooms (Hmm, under the big portrait of John Wayne? Or maybe one of the smaller ones?) and watch the characters file in. You'll want some food, of course: a green-chile–smothered breakfast burrito filled with crispy hash browns, or a grilled hamburger, or one of the signature cinnamon rolls, a deadly amalgam of flour, sugar, and some addictive drug that compels you to eat them despite the hydrogenated goo they're swimming in.

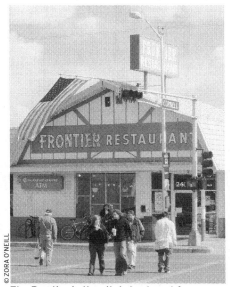

The Frontier is the city's best spot for green-chile stew and people-watching.

If you feel a little unhealthy, you can always get some fresh orange juice and restore your balance by vegging out in front of the mesmerizing tortilla machine.

Near the university, **El Patio** (142 Harvard Dr. SE, 505/268-4245, 11 A.M.–9 P.M. Sun.–Thurs., 11 A.M.–9:30 P.M. Fri. and Sat., $9) is the kind of old-reliable place that ex-locals get misty-eyed about after they've moved away. The green-chile-and-chicken enchiladas are high on many citywide favorite lists. It doesn't hurt that the setting, in an old bungalow with a shady outdoor space, feels like an extension of someone's home kitchen. The menu is more vegetarian-friendly than most New Mexican joints.

All sleek black and silver inside, stylish **Nob Hill Bar & Grill** (3128 Central Ave. SE, 505/266-4455, 11 A.M.–10 P.M. Tues.–Thurs., 11 A.M.–11 P.M. Fri. and Sat., noon–9 P.M. Sun.) does fancified bar food, with hardly anything over $20 (or "20 bucks," in the folksy menu's parlance), and familiar dishes get a little twist of fancy: a crab BLT, for instance, or steak *frites* with a trio of homemade ketchups; salads are only "7 bucks."

Asian

The food at **StreetFood Asia** (3422 Central Ave. SE, 505/260-0088, 11 A.M.–10 P.M. Sun.–Thurs., 11 A.M.–11 P.M. Fri. and Sat., $13) may not be as mind-blowing as it is in Asia, but there's something about its interior, with various cooking stations and lots of plastic, that does conjure a Bangkok mall food court. You can order noodles and other staples prepared in Thai, Vietnamese, Malaysian, and other styles. Two major pluses: the authentic (and authentically weird) shaved-ice-and-bean dessert you often get for free, and its late opening hours.

ALBUQUERQUE METRO AREA

Great places to eat are scattered all over the city, often in unlikely looking strip malls. These places are worth making a trip for, or will provide a pick-me-up when you're far afield.

New Mexican

Experts agree: **◖ Mary & Tito's Café** (2711 4th St. NW, 505/344-6266, 9 A.M.–6 P.M. Mon.–Thurs., 9 A.M.–8 P.M. Fri. and Sat., $7) is the place to go for *carne adovada,* the dish of tender pork braised in red chile, particularly good in what they call a Mexican turnover (a stuffed sopaipilla). The meat is flavorful enough to stand alone, but the fruity, bright red-chile sauce, flecked with seeds, is so good you'll want to put it on everything. This place is such a local icon, seemingly untouched since the 1980s (ah, lovely dusty rose vinyl!), it won a James Beard America's Classics award in 2010.

Cruise down by the rail yards south of downtown to find **El Modelo** (1715 2nd St. SW, 505/242-1843, 7 A.M.–7 P.M. daily, $6), a local go-to for a hangover-curing *chicharrón* burrito, chile-smothered spare ribs, or tamales for the whole family. Because it's really a front for a tortilla factory, the flour tortillas are particularly tender, and you can order either a taco or a whole platter of food. If the weather's nice, grab a seat at a picnic table outside and watch the freight trains go by.

Just two blocks from the National Hispanic Cultural Center, popular **◖ Barelas Coffee House** (1502 4th St. SW, 505/843-7577, 7:30 A.M.–3 P.M. Mon.–Fri., 7:30 A.M.–2:30 P.M. Sat., $7) is confusing to the first-timer: The attraction is chile, not coffee—especially the red, which infuses hearty, timeless New Mexican standards like *posole, chicharrones,* and *menudo.* The restaurant occupies several storefronts, and even then there's often a line out the door at lunch. But it's worth the wait—this is timeless food.

Out in Corrales, **Perea's Restaurant & Tijuana Bar** (4590 Corrales Rd., 505/898-2442, 11 A.M.–2 P.M. Mon.–Sat., $7) is open only for lunch, but it's worth scheduling around if you know you'll be out this way. Everything's home-cooked, from Frito pie to *carne adovada.*

Finally, legendary **K & I Diner** (2500 Broadway SE, 505/243-1881, 6 A.M.–3 P.M. daily, $6) serves New Mexican staples and perhaps the most massive meal you will eat anywhere in New Mexico. It's a single dish, the Travis, an enormous burrito (bigger even than the heads of the high-school football players who come here to bulk up) slathered in chile and topped with French fries. You can order a half-Travis, or even a quarter-Travis, but you'd better have a damn good excuse, such as a stapled stomach, if you opt for the eighth-Travis.

Asian

Can't decide what kind of food you're craving? Cruise the aisles of **Talin Market World Food Fare** (88 Louisiana Blvd. SE, 505/266-07206, 8:30 A.M.–8 P.M. Mon.–Sat., 9 A.M.–7 P.M. Sun.), a megamarket stocked with items from Bombay to the United Kingdom. Its Asian stock is the largest, though, and you can get a variety of hot Laotian, Korean, and Filipino lunch items from the small cafeteria section in one corner and sweets such as pumpkin custard from the bakery. There's also a bubble-tea joint next door, and the parking lot draws a few food trucks.

Just across the parking lot from Talin are two excellent Vietnamese places: **Banh Mi Coda** (230-C Louisiana Blvd. SE, 505/232-0085, 8:30 A.M.–7 P.M. Mon.–Sat., $5), which specializes in the baguette sandwiches (try the peppery meatball) and also serves chewy-sweet coconut waffles and other treats. Next door, rather sleek **Café Trang** (230-A Louisiana Blvd. SE, 505/232-6764, 11 A.M.–9 P.M. Mon.–Sat., $9) has the basics, but its largely Vietnamese clientele demands specialty items like *phô* with chewy beef tendon.

Fine Dining

File under Best High-End Meal in a Strip Mall: Chef Jennifer James has been a fixture on Albuquerque's dining scene for years, but it wasn't until she opened **◖ Jennifer James 101** (4615 Menaul Blvd. NE, 505/884-3860, www.jenniferjames101.com, 5–10 P.M. Tues.–Sat., $26) that she finally got a nod from the James Beard Foundation, in a nomination for Best Chef Southwest in 2009. It hasn't gone to her head. Inside, away from the traffic, the place is supremely calm, and your dinner is a confident mix of seasonal ingredients that sound plain on paper but deliver intense flavor: lamb with rhubarb chutney, for instance, or a pasta with fiddlehead ferns and mushrooms. Check the website for special events: occasional prix-fixe "dinner parties" on Sundays, and the Wednesday "community table." For $35 for three family-style courses, it's a bargain, and a social treat for solo travelers. You must reserve ahead at all times.

Outside Albuquerque

In every direction from the city are great natural attractions. To the west, on land that looks like a movie backdrop, lies Acoma, an ancient pueblo that seems to have grown out of the tall mesa on which it's built. Southeast of town, a winding road through the mountains brings you past the ruined Salinas Pueblo Missions—an intriguing, little-visited bit of early Conquest history. South along I-40, the Rio Grande continues through its fertile valley to the Bosque del Apache, a lush network of marshlands maintained for migrating birdlife; the drive down is a long one, but you can make a day of it with stops at out-of-the-way eateries and a scenic dirt road back. To the east is the start of one of three routes to Santa Fe, the Turquoise Trail, which leads through the vestiges of New Mexico's mining past. An equally scenic route north is the more circuitous Jemez Mountain Trail, past red rocks and hot springs. Or you can zip directly up the main highway, where you'll pass the windswept region known as Tent Rocks.

WEST TO ACOMA

I-40 climbs the West Mesa out of Albuquerque and heads dead straight across a plateau lined with flat mesas—archetypal Southwest scenery. Although it's somewhat dull freeway driving, the trip out this way is well worth it, as ancient Acoma Pueblo is built on top of one of these mesas, an amazing place to visit and meet the people whose ancestors have lived here for nearly a thousand years.

Laguna Pueblo

About 18 miles west of Albuquerque, I-40 crosses the border onto the 45 square miles of Laguna Pueblo (505/552-6654, www.lagunapueblo.org), on which nearly 8,000 Keresan-speaking Ka-waikah (Lake People) live in six villages. From the highway, the only impression you get of Laguna is its Dancing Eagle Casino, but if you have time, get off at exit 114 to visit the **San José Mission Church.** Established in 1699 when the Laguna people requested a priest (unlike any other pueblo), it stands out for its stark white stucco coating, but this is a relatively recent addition, following a 19th-century renovation. It was mudded and whitewashed every year until the 1950s, when the boom in uranium mining in the area left no time for this maintenance; it's now sealed with stucco.

Inside, between a packed-earth floor and a finely wrought wood ceiling, the late-18th-century altar screen commands the full focus of the room. It's the work of the so-called "Laguna Santero," an unidentified painter who made the innovation of placing icons inside a crowded field of decorative borders and carved and painted columns, creating a work of explosively colorful folk art that was copied elsewhere in the region in subsequent decades.

If you're lucky, **Alfred Pino**, a local artist and informal guide, will be hanging around the church and offer you a personal tour and explanation of the symbols on the altar and the painted elk hides on the walls, in exchange for a tip and donation to the church. The church is officially open 8 A.M. to 4:30 P.M. weekdays (after a 7 A.M. morning Mass), but it's often open later and on weekends if Alfred's around.

Each of the six villages of Laguna celebrates its own feast day, and then the whole pueblo turns out at the church September 17–19 for the Feast of San José, one of the bigger pueblo events in the Albuquerque area. Along with traditional dances and an arts-and-crafts market, the pueblo hosts the All-Indian Baseball Tournament, in which the very sports-minded pueblo fields five semipro teams.

◖ ACOMA PUEBLO

At Exit 102 off I-40, visitors to Acoma turn south. The road soon crosses up and over a ridge, and you may feel as though you've crossed through a pass into a Southwestern Shangri-La, for none of this great basin is visible from the highway. Down in the valley, the route runs directly toward a flat-topped rock that juts up like a tooth.

Atop this rock is the original Acoma Pueblo, the village known as Sky City. The community covers about 70 acres and is built entirely of pale, sun-bleached adobe, as it has been since at least 1100. Only 50 or so people live on the mesa top year-round, given the hardships of no running water or electricity, but many families maintain homes here, and the place is thronged on September 2, when the pueblo members gather for the **Feast of San Esteban.** The rest of the 2,800 Acoma (People of the White Rock, in their native Keresan) live on the valley floor, which is used primarily as ranchland.

Visiting Sky City

The fragile nature of the windswept village accounts in part for the particularly stringent tourism policies. All visitors must stop at the **Sky City Cultural Center and Haak'u Museum** (Indian Rte. 23, 800/747-0181, www.acomaskycity.org, 9 A.M.–5 P.M. daily March–mid-Nov., 9 A.M.–5 P.M. Fri.–Sun. mid-Nov.–Feb.) on the main road, which houses a café and shop stocked with local crafts, along with beautiful rotating exhibits on Acoma art and tradition. From here, you must join a guided tour ($20), which transports groups by bus to the village. The one concession to modernity has been the carving of this road to the top;

© ZORA O'NEILL

descending into the valley toward Acoma Pueblo

previously, all goods had to be hauled up the near-vertical cliff faces. The tour lasts about an hour and a half, after which visitors may return by bus or hike down one of the old trails, using hand- and footholds dug into the rock centuries ago. In summer, tours start at 9:30 A.M. and depart every 45 minutes or so, with the last one going at 3:30 P.M. In the winter, the first tour begins at 10:15 A.M., and they go about hourly until 3 P.M. Any time, it's a good idea to call ahead and verify times.

The centerpiece of the village is the **Church of San Esteban del Rey,** one of the most iconic of the Spanish missions in New Mexico. Built between 1629 and 1640, the graceful, simple structure has been inspiring New Mexican architects ever since. (Visitors are not allowed inside, however, or into the adjoining cemetery.) As much as it represents the pinnacle of Hispano-Indian architecture in the 17th century, it's also a symbol of the brutality of Spanish colonialism, as it rose in the typical way: forced labor. The men of Acoma felled and carried the tree trunks for the ceiling beams from the forest on Mount Taylor, more than 25 miles across the valley, and up the cliff face to the village.

Acoma is well known for its pottery, easily distinguished by the fine black lines that sweep around the curves of the creamy-white vessel. On the best works, the lines are so fine and densely painted, they shimmer almost like a moiré. The clay particular to this area can be worked extremely thin to create a pot that will hum or ring when you tap it. Throughout the village, you have opportunities to buy samples. Given the constraints of the tour, this can feel slightly pressured, but in many cases, you have the privilege of buying a piece directly from the artisan who created it.

Accommodations and Food
The cultural center contains the **Y'aak'a Café** (11 A.M.–4:30 P.M. daily, $8), which serves earthy local dishes like lamb stew, tamales, and corn roasted in a traditional *horno* oven—as well as Starbucks coffee. Acoma Pueblo operates the small-scale **Sky City Casino & Hotel**

(877/552-6123, www.skycity.com, $59 d), also at exit 102. Its rooms are perfectly functional and very well priced if you book online, and there's a nice pool.

SALINAS PUEBLO MISSIONS NATIONAL MONUMENT
Set on the plains behind the Manzano Mountains, the scenically decaying mud-brick buildings at Quarai, Gran Quivira, and Abó represent one of the Franciscans' bigger challenges during the early years of the Conquest. The national monument designation applies to three separate sites. Visiting them all takes a full day, and the route (Highway 337, beginning in Tijeras, just east of the city) also passes by the little town of Mountainair, as well as one of the area's most beautiful fall hiking spots.

Tijeras
To reach Highway 337, take I-40 east to exit 179. Settled in the 1850s, the village of Tijeras

a warren of interconnected rooms at Gran Quivira

the ruins at Abó

(Scissors, for the way the canyons meet here) is still a stronghold of old Hispano traditions, though it doesn't look too distinctive on the surface. Beginning the ascent along the mountains, you soon pass the **Ponderosa Steakhouse** (10676 Hwy. 337, 505/281-8278, 11 A.M.–9 P.M. Tues.–Sat., 9 A.M.–9 P.M. Sun., $15), which is really more of a bar, populated by mountain men far more grizzled than you'd expect this close to the big city. But the steak (and especially the steak fajitas) is good and inexpensive—you could drive the route backward if you want to end with dinner here.

Fourth of July Canyon

Past the Spanish land grant of Chililí (its terms have been contested ever since the Treaty of Guadalupe Hidalgo), Highway 337 runs into Highway 55—make a right and head to Tajique, then turn onto Forest Road 55 to reach Fourth of July Canyon. The area in the foothills of the Manzanos, seven miles down the dirt road, is a destination in late September and early October, when the red maples and

oak trees turn every shade of pink, crimson, and orange imaginable. (Actually, the place got its name not for this fireworks-like show of colors, but for the date an Anglo explorer happened across it in 1906.) It's also pretty in late summer, when the rains bring wildflowers. You can explore on the short **Spring Loop Trail** or **Crimson Maple Trail,** or really get into the woods on **Fourth of July Trail** (no. 173), which wanders into the canyon 1.8 miles and connects with **Albuquerque Trail** (no. 78) to form a loop.

Forest Road 55 loops back to meet Highway 55, but the second half, after the campground, can be very rough going. It's usually maintained in the fall, but at other times of the year, it's wiser to backtrack rather than carry on, especially if you're in a rental car.

Quarai

The first ruins you reach are those at Quarai (505/847-2290, www.nps.gov/sapu, 9 A.M.–6 P.M. daily June–Aug., 9 A.M.–5 P.M. Sept.–May, free), a pueblo inhabited from the 14th to the 17th centuries. Like the other two Salinas pueblos, Quarai was a hardscrabble place with no natural source of water and very little food, though it did act as a trading outpost for salt, brought from small salt lakes farther east (hence the name). When the Franciscans arrived, then, they put more than the usual strain on this community of 400 or so Tiwa speakers; they nonetheless managed to build a grand sandstone-and-adobe mission, the most impressive of the ones at these three pueblos. In addition to a struggle with the local population, the priests found themselves at odds with the Spanish governors, who helped protect them but also undermined their conversion work by encouraging ceremonial dances. At the same time, raids by Apaches increased because any crop surplus no longer went to them in trade, but to the Spanish. *And* there were terrible famines between 1663 and 1670. No wonder, then, that the place was abandoned even before the Pueblo Revolt of 1680. Only the mission has been excavated; the surrounding hillocks are all pueblo structures.

Mountainair

Highway 55 meets U.S. 60 in the village of Mountainair, which hosts the **Salinas Pueblo Missions Visitors Center** (505/847-2585, www.nps.gov/sapu, 8 A.M.–5 P.M. daily), on U.S. 60 west of the intersection—though it offers not much more information than what's available at the small but detailed museums at each site. The **Mountainair ranger station** (505/847-2990, 8 A.M.–noon and 12:30–4:30 P.M. Mon.–Fri.) is also here, for those who want trail maps for the Manzanos and the like. Coming from the north, follow signs west off Highway 55, before you reach the U.S. 60 intersection.

Mountainair is also home to the weird architectural treasure that is the **Shaffer Hotel** (103 Main St., 505/847-2888, www.shafferhotel.com), a 1923 Pueblo Deco confection with a folk-art twist, built by one Clem "Pop" Shaffer, who had a way with cast concrete—look for his name in the wall enclosing the little garden. Redone in late 2005, the hotel has unfortunately not been kept up well, and its rooms

© ZORA O'NEILL

Folk artist "Pop" Shaffer was highly creative with rocks.

(from just $28 for one with a shared bath) are recommended only if you have a chance to inspect them first—don't reserve ahead. Better to stop in just for a snack or a drink at the adjacent **Pack's Café** (6 A.M.–8 P.M. Mon.–Sat., 8 A.M.–5 P.M. Sun.), where the wood ceiling is Shaffer's masterpiece: intricately carved and painted, it crawls with turtles, snakes, and other critters.

For real sustenance, hit bustling **Alpine Alley** (210 N. Summit Ave., 505/847-2478, 6 A.M.–2 P.M. Mon.–Fri., 8 A.M.–2 P.M. Sat.), just north of the main intersection on Highway 55. This café is the town living room, serving good baked treats, soups, and creative sandwiches and drinks to a crew of regulars, many of whom have inspired the menu's concoctions.

Gran Quivira

South from Mountainair 26 miles lies Gran Quivira—a bit of a drive, and you'll have to backtrack, but on the way you'll pass **Rancho Bonito,** another Pop Shaffer creation—his actual home. As it's private property, you can't go poking around, but from the road you can see a bit of the little log cabin painted in black, red, white, and blue. (If you happen to be in Mountainair in May for its art tour, the house is open for tours then.)

Where Highway 55 makes a sharp turn east, Gran Quivira (505/847-2770, www.nps.gov/sapu, 9 A.M.–6 P.M. daily June–Aug., 9 A.M.–5 P.M. Sept.–May, free) looks different from the other two Salinas pueblos because it is built of gray San Andres limestone slabs, not sandstone, and finished with plaster that was painted with symbols. It's the largest of three, with an estimated population between 1,500 and 2,000, likely devoted to trade, as the large array of feathers and pottery styles found here indicate. Like the people of Abó, the residents spoke Tompiro, and the Spanish dubbed them Los Rayados, for the striped decorations they wore on their faces. It appears they outwardly accepted the Franciscan mission after the first sermon was preached here in 1627. But they took their own religion literally underground, building hidden kivas underneath the residential structures even as they toiled on two successive missions ordered by the Catholics. Nonetheless, the place was deserted by 1671, after more than a third of the population had starved to death.

Abó

From Gran Quivira, drive back the way you came and turn west on U.S. 60 in Mountainair to reach Abó (505/847-2400, www.nps.gov/sapu, free), nine miles on. The visitors center here has the same hours as the other sites (9 A.M.–6 P.M. daily June–Aug., 9 A.M.–5 P.M. Sept.–May, free), but the ruins themselves are open all the time—it's nice to drop by here just as the setting sun is lending a red glow to the rocks. Abó was the first pueblo the Franciscans visited, in 1622; the mission here, constructed over more than 60 years, shows details such as old wood stairs leading to the choir loft. (The Franciscans were so dedicated to re-creating the Catholic church experience here in the desert that they brought in portable pipe organs and trained their converts to sing.)

Unlike Gran Quivira, though, Abó seems to have had some agreement regarding kivas, as there is one built right in the center of the *convento* (the compound adjoining the mission), dating from the same period—something that no archaeologist or historian has yet explained. The excellent condition of all of these ruins is due in part to a family that owned the land from the mid-19th century on—one member, Federico Sisneros, is buried near the mission, at his request.

From Abó, you can continue west through the mountain pass, then down into the long, flat Rio Grande valley on U.S. 60, which runs straight into I-25 at Bernardo. If you're heading back to Albuquerque, you can take Highway 47 northwest to Belén, about 25 miles closer to the city.

SOUTH TO THE BOSQUE DEL APACHE

If you haven't gotten enough of the area's birdlife along the Rio Grande in the city, head to the Bosque del Apache bird sanctuary, which is the site of an awe-inspiring fly-in of giant sandhill cranes during November and hosts hundreds of other migratory species in the fall and winter. On the way there or back, you can strike out into truly remote New Mexico along the Quebradas Scenic Byway.

Socorro

Once a pueblo that offered food to conquistador Don Juan de Oñate, Socorro (Succor, or Relief) now shelters the students of the **New Mexico Institute of Mining & Technology** (a.k.a. New Mexico Tech, 575/835-5011, www.nmt.edu), which has been training engineers since 1889. The town has a small time-warp historic plaza, but the mission-style campus is scenic as well. To reach it, turn west from the main north–south route, California Street, onto Bullock Street and follow it toward the hills.

Wet your whistle at the **Capitol Bar** (575/835-1193, noon–2 A.M. Mon.–Sat., noon–midnight Sun.) on the plaza, which doesn't seem to have changed much in its century of doing business—this is one of those dim, swinging-door saloons that you thought existed only in movie sets. **M Mountain Coffee** (110 Manzanares St., 575/838-0809, 7 A.M.–8 P.M. daily), just off the plaza, is a popular non-alcoholic hangout, with gelato and breakfast as well.

For a full meal, try **Socorro Springs** (1012 N. California St., 575/838-0650, 10:30 A.M.–10 P.M. daily, $11), a brewpub on the north end of the main drag through town with a diverse menu, from morning coffee and omelets through late-night flame-grilled burgers and creative pizzas. Another local favorite is **Ⓒ Frank & Lupe's El Sombrero** (210 Mesquite St. NE, 575/835-3945, 11 A.M.–9 P.M. daily, $7), where the salsa verde is tangy, the tamales are appropriately rich with lard, and the airy interior courtyard is pretty and relaxing. It's just east of I-25 on the north side (exit 150).

As for accommodations, chain motels are the only real options here—the **Motel 6** (807 S. U.S. 85, 575/835-3500, www.motel6.com,

$34 d) on the south side is basic but fine for overnight, and the **Holiday Inn Express** (1040 N. California St., 888/465-4329, www.hiexpress.com, $109 d) is positively plush.

San Antonio

Even though it's just a blip on the map, this town supports two great burger joints: the **Ⓒ Owl Bar & Café** (U.S. 380, 575/835-9946, 8 A.M.–8:15 P.M. Mon.–Sat., $6), which has always gotten all the press, and the lesser-known **Manny's Buckhorn** (U.S. 380, 575/835-4423, 11 A.M.–8 P.M. Mon.–Fri., 11 A.M.–2:45 P.M. Sat., $6), just across the street. Both serve beer and green-chile cheeseburgers, both have chummy local staff and plenty of lore—so how to choose? Go to the Owl if you like your burgers thin, to Manny's if you like them a little fatter. Actually, the Owl gets an extra point for historic detail: The bar here is from the world's first Hilton hotel—not part of Conrad Hilton's international chain, but the one opened by his father when he moved here in the 1880s; Conrad was born shortly thereafter, grew up to be his father's business partner, and went on to develop hotel properties around the world. The Owl's owners salvaged the bar after the structure surrounding it burned.

If you want to wake up and get straight to the birds, **Casa Blanca B&B** (13 Montoya St., 575/835-3027, www.casablancabedandbreakfast.com, $80 d) can put you up for the night in one of three cozy rooms in an 1880 Victorian farmhouse; it's closed June–September. You can camp at the **Bosque Birdwatchers RV Park** (575/835-1366, $15), just 100 yards north of the reserve border on Highway 1.

Bosque del Apache National Wildlife Refuge

Occupying 57,191 acres on either side of the Rio Grande, this bird sanctuary is in a sense a manufactured habitat: Controlled flooding creates the marshes that draw the birds, which find food on farm plots dedicated to tasty grains. But this is really restoring a process that happened naturally before the Rio Grande was dammed. The birds certainly

COURTESY ALBUQUERQUE CVB / © DICK THOMPSON

Migrating birds settle in for the winter at Bosque del Apache National Wildlife Refuge.

have no objection. Arctic geese, sandhill cranes, bald eagles, and a whole variety of ducks happily settle in for the winter. In the spring, migratory warblers and pelicans stop off on their way back to points north, while great blue herons make their spring nests here. Summer is relatively quiet, as only the year-round species remain: hummingbirds, swallows, flycatchers, and the like.

Five miles inside the north border of the reserve, you pass the **visitors center** (575/835-1828, 7:30 A.M.–4 P.M. Mon.–Fri., 8 A.M.–4:30 P.M. Sat. and Sun.), where you can pick up maps and find out which birds have been spotted that day. A bit farther south on Highway 1, a 12-mile paved car loop passes through all the marshlands and the grain fields; at certain points along the drive, you can get out and hike set trails, such as a quarter-mile boardwalk across a lagoon or a trail to the river. Some areas are open to mountain bikers. The loop drive opens when birdlife is at its best, one hour before sunrise; cars need to be out by an hour after dark. With all its

marshland, the *bosque* could just as well be called a mosquito sanctuary—slather on plenty of repellent before you start your drive.

The biggest event of the year is the arrival of the sandhill cranes—they were the inspiration for the refuge, as their population had dwindled to fewer than 20 in 1941. But now more than 15,000 of these graceful birds with six-foot wingspans winter over in the *bosque*. They're celebrated annually at the five-day **Festival of the Cranes** (www.friendsofthe-bosque.org) in November, when birders gather to witness the mass morning liftoffs and evening fly-ins.

Quebradas Backcountry Byway

This 24-mile dirt road runs in a jagged arc from U.S. 380 up to I-25 north of Socorro. Along the way, it cuts across several deep arroyos, or natural drainage channels—these are the *quebradas* ("breaks") in the earth that give the area its name. The rounded hills here are striped with rainbow hues, and the scrub desert teems with hawks, mule deer, and foxes.

The route makes a good slow way back to Albuquerque if you've come down early in the morning to see the birds (though you could just as easily drive down this way and hit the *bosque* near sunset). The drive takes between two and three hours on a good day. This is remote wilderness—be sure you have extra food and water, as well as a spare tire. Don't attempt it if it has rained very recently, as the mud can be impossible to pass, and look out for sandy patches at all times.

From the intersection of the *bosque* road (Highway 1) in San Antonio, in front of the Owl Café, head east on U.S. 380 for just over 10 miles; then turn north on County Road A-129, the beginning of the byway. Coming from Albuquerque is a little trickier: Leave I-25 at Escondida (exit 152), then go north for 1.3 miles on the east-side frontage road; turn east at Escondida Lake and continue for 0.8 mile, crossing the river, to Pueblito, where you turn right at a T intersection. After about a mile, you'll see a sign for the byway beginning on your left (west);

the road ends on U.S. 380 about 10 miles east of San Antonio and the road to the *bosque.*

THE TURQUOISE TRAIL

This scenic back route to Santa Fe, which runs along the east side of the Sandias and up across high plateaus, revisits New Mexico's mining history as it passes through a series of ghost towns. Take I-40 east from Albuquerque to exit 175. If you want to pick up hiking maps of the area, bear right to go into the village of Tijeras and the **Sandia ranger station** (11776 Hwy. 337, 505/281-3304). Go left to continue directly to the junction with Highway 14, the beginning of the Turquoise Trail.

◖ Tinkertown Museum

The four-lane road heads north through alternating communities of old Spanish land grants and modern subdivisions collectively referred to as the East Mountains. Six miles on, you come to a large triangle intersection—to the left is Highway 536, the Crest Road up to Sandia Peak, a beautiful winding

wise words from Ross Ward, who built Tinkertown

drive through steadily thinning forests until you reach the exposed top of the mountain, more than 10,000 feet above sea level and more than 5,500 feet above the center of Albuquerque. Even if you don't drive to the crest, do head 1.5 miles up the Crest Road to Tinkertown Museum (505/281-5233, 9 A.M.–6 P.M. daily Apr.–Oct., $3), a temple to efficient use of downtime.

Ross Ward, an artist and sign painter who learned his trade doing banners for carnivals, was also a master whittler and creative engineer who built, over 40 years, thousands of elaborate miniature figures and dioramas out of wood, some of which he even animated with tiny pulleys and levers: a man with a cleaver chases chickens in a circle, circus performers soar, the blacksmith's bellows huff and puff. Many of the buildings themselves are Ward's creations as well—undulating walls made of bottles and studded with odd collectibles, for instance. The museum, like an amoeba, even seems to have taken over a friend and neighbor's 35-foot wooden boat. Ward died in 2002; his family keeps up the museum, and even though it's no longer growing as it used to, it remains a remarkable piece of pure folk art.

Golden

Back on Highway 14, continue north through rolling hills and ever-broader sky. After 15 miles, you reach the all-but-gone town of Golden—so named because it was the site of the first gold strike west of the Mississippi, in 1825. But all that's left now is a handful of homes, an attractive adobe church, and **Henderson Store** (10 A.M.–3:30 P.M. Tues.–Sat.), a general store open since 1918. It's largely given over to Indian jewelry and pottery, and antique trinkets line the upper shelves, remnants of Golden's moment of glory. One other small attraction: the house across the road, bedecked with thousands of antique bottles.

Madrid

Thirteen miles beyond Golden, and about midway along the drive, Madrid (pronounced MAD-rid) is a ghost town back from the dead.

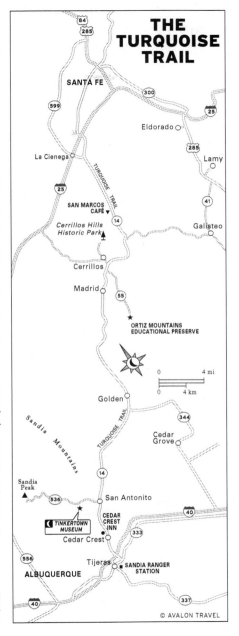

THE TURQUOISE TRAIL

© AVALON TRAVEL

BIRDING ON THE PEAK

Sandia Peak in the dead of winter does not seem hospitable to life in any form, much less flocks of delicate-looking birds the size of your fist, fluffing around cheerfully in the frigid air. But that's precisely what you'll see if you visit in the iciest months, particularly right after a big snowfall. The feathered critters in question are rosy finches, a contrary, cold-loving variety (sometimes called "refrigerator birds") that migrate from as far north as the Arctic tundra between November and March to the higher elevations of New Mexico, which must seem relatively tropical by comparison.

What's special about Sandia is that it draws all three species of rosy finch, which in turn draws dedicated birders looking to add the finches to their life lists. *Birder's World* magazine praises Sandia Peak as "the world's most accessible location to see all three species of rosy finches." This is a boon for people who are more accustomed to kayaking through swamps and slogging through tropical forests to spot rare species. So if you see the finches—they're midsize brown or black birds with pink bellies, rumps, and wings—you'll probably also spy some human finch fans. But they might not have time to talk, as it's not unheard-of for the most obsessive birders – those on their "big year," out to spot as many species as possible in precisely 365 days – to fly in to Albuquerque, drive to the crest, eyeball the finches, and drive right back down and fly out in search of even more obscure varieties.

Built by the Albuquerque & Cerrillos Coal Co. in 1906, it once housed 4,000 people, but it was deserted by the end of World War II, when natural gas became more widespread. By the late 1970s, a few of the swaybacked wood houses had been reoccupied by hippies who were willing to live where indoor plumbing was barely available. Over the decades, Madrid slowly revived. Portable toilets are still more common than flush models, but the arts scene has flourished, and a real sense of community pervades the main street, which is lined with galleries and pretty painted bungalows. In 2006, the village was the setting for the John Travolta film *Wild Hogs,* and the set-piece café built for the production (now a souvenir shop) has become a minor pilgrimage site for bikers.

You can learn more about Madrid's history at the **Old Coal Town Museum** (Hwy. 14, 505/438-3780, www.themineshafttavern.com, 11 A.M.–5 P.M. Fri.–Mon., $5), where you can wander among sinister-looking machine parts and even walk partway down an abandoned mineshaft—a great disciplinary tool for kids who've been acting up in the car. You'll feel the "ghost" in "ghost town" here. There's an Old West costume photo studio in the lobby, and,

if it ever gets revamped to meet fire codes, the melodrama-ready **Engine House Theatre**—check the website for updates.

A more vibrant remnant of Madrid's company-town days is the **Mine Shaft Tavern** (2846 Hwy. 14, 505/473-0743, 11:30 A.M.–10 P.M. daily), where you can belly up to a 40-foot-long pine-pole bar. Above it are murals by local artist Ross Ward, who built the Tinkertown Museum in Sandia Park. "It is better to drink than to work," reads the Latin inscription interwoven among the mural panels, and certainly everyone in the bar, from long-distance bikers to gallery-hoppers, is living by those encouraging words.

For coffee and local gossip, hit **Java Junction** (2855 Hwy. 14, 505/438-2772, www.javajunction.com, from 7:30 A.M. daily), which also rents a **guest room** ($109 d). For more substance, head straight to **Mama Lisa's Ghost Town Kitchen** ($10). When it's open (seemingly not on a regular basis, but chances are better in the summer), it's a true treat, a cozy place with an all-over-the-map menu: bison enchiladas, Austrian-style pork chops, lemon butter cake, and hibiscus mint tea, which you can enjoy out on the tree-shaded front patio. When it's closed, all you can do is press

It's not really a diner — it's a set from *Wild Hogs*, now housing a souvenir shop.

your face against the window and dream—or go down the street to **The Hollar** (Hwy. 14, 575/471-4821, 11 A.M.–7 P.M. Mon.–Wed., 11 A.M.–9 P.M. Thurs.–Sun., $9), which dishes out fancied-up Southern standards like po' boys, fried green tomatoes, and ooey-gooey cheese grits—it's casual by day and more refined in the evening, making it the kind of place Santa Feans drive to for a treat. The last resort—though not a bad option at all—is the food at the **Mine Shaft Tavern:** "roadhouse cuisine," including green-chile cheeseburgers. The kitchen closes at 7:30 P.M. weeknights and 9 P.M. on Friday and Saturday.

Ortiz Mountains Educational Preserve

This 1,350-acre reserve, managed by the Santa Fe Botanical Garden (505/471-9103, www.santafebotanicalgarden.org), is open by guided tour only. Organized walks ($5 donation) on weekends usually last a few hours, and they wind through the piñon scrub for viewing local plants or discussing mining history in the area. The reserve is about six miles down County Road 55.

Cerrillos

By contrast with Madrid, Cerrillos, said to be the source of turquoise that has been traced to Chaco Canyon, Spain, and Chichén Itzá in Mexico's Yucatán Peninsula, hasn't been gallerified like its neighbor down the road. There's a couple of antiques stores (one ghostly, one better dusted), plus a combo **petting zoo-trading post** with a llama and a sheep, plus turquoise nuggets and taxidermied jackalopes. And there's one barely bar, **Mary's,** filled with cats and serving as more of a sitting room for the proprietress and namesake, who's in her 10th decade. All this means it's a pretty quiet place to wake up, at the artfully decorated **Cerrillos Hills B&B** (12 3rd St., 505/424-3125, www.cerrilloshillsbedandbreakfast.com), which has one large suite ($124) and a stand-alone guesthouse ($139) on a tree-shaded back street.

If you want to do something besides wave to the Amtrak train in the afternoon, you can go **horseback riding** (Broken Saddle Riding Co., 505/424-7774, www.brokensaddle.com, $80 for two hours) or hiking in **Cerrillos Hills**

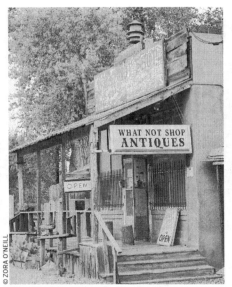

The What Not Shop in Cerrillos is perhaps the dustiest antiques store in the state.

State Park (head north across the railroad tracks, www.nmparks.com, $5/car), more than 1,000 acres of rolling hills and narrow canyons that are also good for mountain biking.

The Home Stretch

After ascending from the canyons around Cerrillos onto a high plateau (look out for antelope), you're on the home stretch to Santa Fe—but you'll pass one more dining option, the **San Marcos Café** (3877 Hwy. 14, 505/471-9298, 8 a.m.–2 p.m. daily, $9), which shares space with a working feed store where chickens scratch in the yard. Breakfast in the country-style dining room (a potbellied stove lurks in one corner) is especially delicious, with great cinnamon buns, homemade chicken sausage, and a variety of egg dishes.

From here, Highway 14 continues on to become Cerrillos Road, the very slow and unscenic way into Santa Fe. The more direct route is via I-25 to Old Santa Fe Trail. Keep an eye out for the highway on-ramp—signs point to Las Vegas.

THE JEMEZ MOUNTAIN TRAIL

Beginning just northwest of Albuquerque, the Jemez (HAY-mez) Mountain Trail is an exceptionally beautiful drive, as it passes through Jemez Indian Reservation, the Santa Fe National Forest, and the Valles Caldera National Preserve. It's the least direct way of getting to Santa Fe—you actually wind up near Los Alamos and must backtrack a bit south to reach town—but nature lovers will want to set aside a full day for the trip, which is especially beautiful in the fall, when the aspen leaves turn vivid yellow against the rich red rocks. The drive begins on U.S. 550, which goes northwest out of the satellite town of Bernalillo, just west of I-25. At the village of San Ysidro, bear right onto Highway 4, which forms the major part of the route north.

Jemez Pueblo

This community of some 3,000 tribal members settled in the area in the late 13th century, and Highway 4 runs through the middle of the 89,000 acres it still maintains. Before the Spanish arrived, the Hemish people (which the Spanish spelled *Jemez*) had established more than 10 large villages in the area. The pueblo is quite conservative and closed to outsiders except for ceremonial dances. Because Jemez absorbed members of Pecos Pueblo in 1838, it celebrates two feast days, San Diego (November 12) and San Persingula (August 2). It's also the only remaining pueblo where residents speak the Towa language, the rarest of the related New Mexico languages (Tewa and Tiwa are the other two). The pueblo operates the **Walatowa Visitors Center** (575/834-7235, www.jemezpueblo.org, 8 a.m.–5 p.m. daily Apr.–Dec., 10 a.m.–4 p.m. Jan.–Mar.), about five miles north of San Ysidro. The center is easy to miss because you'll be gawking at the east side of the road at the lurid red sandstone cliffs at the mouth of the **San Diego Canyon.** From April till October, another, tastier distraction is the Indian frybread and enchiladas sold by roadside vendors. The visitors center has exhibits about the local geology and the people of Jemez and doubles as a

© ZORA O'NEILL

Stop for fresh frybread at Jemez Pueblo.

ranger station, dispensing maps and advice on outdoor recreation farther up the road—including the status of trails, campgrounds, and fishing access points following the Las Conchas fire in 2011. You can take a one-mile guided hike ($5) up into the red rocks; it's a good idea to call ahead and arrange a time.

Jemez Springs

This charming small resort town—really just a handful of little clapboard buildings tucked in the narrow valley along the road—is the most convenient place to indulge in some of the area's springs, which are a stew of minerals and trace elements like lithium that have inspired tales of miraculous healing since people began visiting in the 1870s. **Giggling Springs** (Hwy. 4, 575/829-9175, www.gigglingsprings.com, 11 A.M.–sunset Tues.–Sun., $17/hour or $48/day), built in the 1880s, has a spring-fed pool enclosed in an attractively landscaped flagstone area right near the Jemez River. In winter, it's open only Wednesday–Sunday. The **Jemez Springs Bath House** (Hwy. 4, 575/829-3303,

www.jemezsprings.org, 10 A.M.–7 P.M. daily, $18 per hour) is operated by the village. Here, the springs have been diverted into eight soaking tubs. They're private, but they have a somewhat austere feel. Call ahead to reserve; massages and other spa treatments are available as well.

For a bite to eat and a place to stay, **Laughing Lizard Inn & Café** (Hwy. 4, 575/829-3108, www.thelaughinglizard.com, $70 d) offers four basic but pretty rooms opening onto a long porch. The café occupies an old tin-ceiling general store and serves an eclectic menu of Moroccan chicken, pizzas, and fresh salads (about $10). If all that seems too healthy and modern, head to **Los Ojos Restaurant & Saloon** (17596 Hwy. 4, 575/829-3547, 11 A.M.–midnight Mon.–Fri., 8 A.M.–midnight Sat. and Sun., $9), where horseshoes double as window grills, tree trunks act as barstools, and the atmosphere hasn't changed in decades. Burgers are the way to go. The kitchen shuts around 9 P.M., and bar closing time can come earlier if business is slow, so call ahead in the evenings.

If you're planning to explore the wilderness and missed the Walatowa Visitors Center at Jemez Pueblo, you can stop at the **Jemez Ranger District Office** (Hwy. 4, 575/829-3535, 8 A.M.–5 P.M. Mon.–Fri.) for info. There's a **visitors center for Valles Caldera National Preserve** (Hwy. 4, 575/661-3333, 8 A.M.–5 P.M. Mon.–Fri.) here too—stop in to arrange reservations for the park or to see if there are last-minute openings. Both are on the north edge of town.

Jemez State Monument

Just north of Jemez Springs, you pass this set of ruins (Hwy. 4, 575/829-3530, 8:30 A.M.–5 P.M. Wed.–Sun., $3), where the ancestors of the present Jemez people settled more than 700 years ago and lived until the Pueblo Revolt of 1680. More striking than the old pueblo, which was named Giusewa, is the crumbling Franciscan mission that rises up in the middle of it. The convent and church of San José de los Jémez were built around 1620, using forced labor from the pueblo; the result was remarkably lavish, but the friars had abandoned their work by 1640, probably because they'd thoroughly antagonized their would-be parishioners. Today the remnants of the two different cultures have nearly dissolved back into the earth from which they were both built, but the church's unique octagonal bell tower has been reconstructed to good effect. Pay $5 admission, and you can also visit Coronado State Monument, on the north edge of Albuquerque, on the same day.

A couple of curves in the highway past the monument, you reach the rocks of **Soda Dam** off the right side of the road. The pale, bulbous mineral accretions that have developed around this spring resemble nothing so much as the top of a root beer float, with a waterfall crashing through the middle. You can't really dip in the water here, but it's a good photo op.

Hot Springs

Outside of the town of Jemez Springs, you pass several other opportunities to take a hot bath. Five miles north, where the red rocks of the canyon have given way to steely-gray stone and Battleship Rock looms above the road, is the trail to **McCauley Springs.** These require a two-mile hike along East Fork Trail (the parking area for the trailhead is just past Battleship Rock Picnic Area) but are an excellent motivator for a not-too-strenuous climb. Follow the trail until it meets a small stream flowing down from your left (north), then walk up the creek about a quarter mile to the spring, which has been diverted so it flows into a series of pools of ever-cooler temperatures (only 85°F at most points). Because the trail runs along the streambed, though, it's usually impassable in the high-flow winter and spring.

The most accessible pools are **Spence Springs,** about half a mile north of Battleship Rock. A sign marks a parking area on the east side of the road, and the trail to the springs starts immediately south of the dirt pullout. A short hike (0.4 mile) leads down to the river then up the steep hillside to two sets of 100°F pools. The place is well known, and although there are signs insisting on clothing, don't be surprised if you encounter some people bathing nude.

Hiking

Several trails run through the Jemez, but damage from the 2011 Las Conchas wildfire has made the ones on the eastern side of the forest less scenic. The western portion of **East Fork Trail** (no. 137) is still quite nice, however. The whole trail runs from Battleship Rock Picnic Area to Las Conchas, crossing Highway 4 in the middle, a convenient midpoint. Heading west from the parking area (about three miles after the highway makes its hairpin turn southeast) takes you to Jemez Falls after 1 mile, and then gradually down to Battleship Rock, in about 6 miles, passing McCauley Springs on the way. Heading east from the parking area is quite scenic, following a stream through a pine forest, though near the end of 4.5 miles, you approach the burned area.

◖ Valles Caldera National Preserve

Spreading out for 89,000 acres to the north of Highway 4, this protected parkland (866/382-5537, www.vallescaldera.gov) is a series of vast green valleys, rimmed by the edges of a volcano that collapsed into a huge bowl millennia ago. At the center is rounded Redondo Peak (11,254 feet). The park was a private ranch, which the U.S. government purchased in 2000. It's managed with the goal of making the area financially self-sustaining, independent of government funds. To this end, use fees are high (starting at $10 per person), and for all but two trails, you must make reservations at least 24 hours ahead online, as there are restrictions on how many people may enter the park each day. The reward is a hike through untouched land, where you will see herds of elk grazing and eagles winging across the huge dome of the sky.

In 2011, the Las Conchas fire burned about 30 percent of the caldera. Fortunately, most of that area was in the easily replenished grasslands. Unfortunately, the burned area also encompasses those two trails you can hike for free and without a reservation (Valle Grande and Coyote Call). So until growth returns, hiking Valles Caldera requires planning ahead. The season is best June–September, and in winter months, the park is open for cross-country skiing. There are also limited elk-hunting and fishing seasons. A full roster of guided activities is available too: group day hikes, full-moon snowshoeing and sleigh rides, overnight winter yurt camping, tracking classes, horseback riding, and more.

Past Valles Caldera, Highway 4 goes into Bandelier National Monument. If you're carrying on to Santa Fe, go through White Rock and join Highway 502, which leads through Pojoaque to U.S. 285, which then goes south to the capital.

THE INTERSTATE TO SANTA FE

The most direct route north to Santa Fe is along I-25, a drive of about 60 miles. The road,

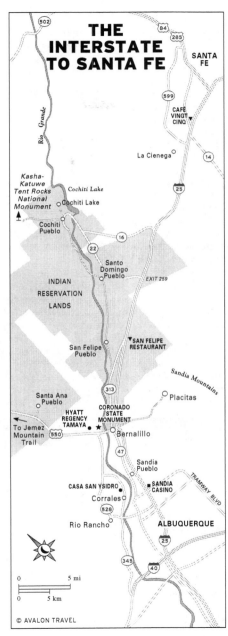

© AVALON TRAVEL

which passes through the broad valley between the Sandia and Jemez mountain ranges, is not as scenic as the more meandering routes, but it does cross wide swaths of undeveloped pueblo lands (Sandia, San Felipe, and Kewa, formerly Santo Domingo).

At exit 252, hop off for a meal at the ◖ **San Felipe Restaurant** (26 Hagan Rd., 505/867-4706, 6 A.M.–9 P.M. daily, $8), alongside a gas station and past a short hall of dinging slot machines. Its broad diner-ish menu of spaghetti and meatballs as well as New Mexican favorites is superlative, especially pueblo dishes like *posole* with extra-thick tortillas. The crowd is just as diverse: pueblo residents, day-trippers, long-haul truckers.

You also have the opportunity to detour to one of the region's most striking natural phenomena, **Kasha-Katuwe Tent Rocks National Monument** (Forest Rd. 266, 7 A.M.–7 P.M. daily mid-Mar.–Oct., 8 A.M.–5 P.M. daily Nov.–mid-Mar., $5/car), where the wind-whittled clusters of volcanic pumice and tuff do indeed resemble enormous tepees, some up to 90 feet tall. To reach the parklands, leave I-25 at exit 259 and head west toward Cochiti Pueblo on Highway 22, then turn south in front of Cochiti Dam, which blots out the horizon around mile 15; before you reach the pueblo, turn right on Indian Route 92. From the monument parking area, you have the choice of two short trails: an easy, relatively flat loop runs up to the base of the rocks, passing a small cave, while a longer option runs 1.5 miles into a narrow canyon where the rock towers loom up dramatically on either side. The latter trail is level at first, but the last stretch is steep and requires a little clambering.

On your way out from the hike, you can drive through **Cochiti Pueblo,** the northernmost Keresan-speaking pueblo, which claims its ancestors inhabited some of the ruins at Bandelier National Monument. The core of the community is still two ancient adobe kivas; the people who live in the surrounding houses sell craftwork. Nearby **Cochiti Lake** (reached by continuing along Highway 22 past the dam) is a popular summer destination for boaters, though it's not particularly scenic.

Finally, just at the edge of Santa Fe is a delectable French café in a most unlikely spot. **Café Vingt Cinq** (8380 Cerrillos Rd., 505/474-7300, 9 A.M.–4 P.M. Mon.–Sat., 9 A.M.–3 P.M. Sun., $7) is tucked in the Fashion Outlets of Santa Fe, an outdoor mall. Avert your eyes from the clearance-sale girdles and tuck in to flawlessly flaky croissants (optionally stuffed with green chile and cheese), tender crepes, and buttery sablé cookies.

Information and Services

TOURIST INFORMATION

The **Albuquerque Convention and Visitors Bureau** (800/284-2282, www.itsatrip.org) offers the most detailed information on the city, maintaining a kiosk on the Old Town plaza in the summer and a desk at the airport near the baggage claim (9:30 A.M.–8 P.M. daily). You can also get excellent information on events at the **Hotel Andaluz,** at the computer terminals on the second-floor mezzanine. The **City of Albuquerque** website (www.cabq.gov) is very well organized, with all the essential details about city-run attractions and services.

Books and Maps

The **University of New Mexico bookstore** (2301 Central Ave. NE, 505/277-5451, 8 A.M.–6 P.M. Mon.–Fri., 10 A.M.–5 P.M. Sat.) maintains a good stock of travel titles and maps, along with state history tomes and the like. On the west side, **Bookworks** (4022 Rio Grande Blvd. NW, 505/344-8139, 9 A.M.–9 P.M. Mon.–Sat., 9 A.M.–7 P.M. Sun.) is a great resource, with a large stock of New Mexico–related work as well as plenty of other titles, all recommended with the personal care of the staff.

Local Media

The *Albuquerque Journal* publishes cultural-events listings in the Friday entertainment supplement. On Wednesdays, pick up the new issue of the free weekly *Alibi* (www.alibi.com), which will give you a hipper, more critical outlook on city goings-on, from art openings to city council debates. The glossy monthly *ABQ The Magazine* (www.abqthemag.com) explores cultural topics, while the free *Local Flavor* (www.localflavormagazine.com) covers food topics.

Radio

KUNM (89.9 FM) is the university's radio station, delivering eclectic music, news from NPR and PRI, and local-interest shows such as *Native America Calling* and *Singing Wire*. **KANW** (89.1 FM) is a project of Albuquerque Public Schools, with an emphasis on New Mexican music of all stripes, but particularly mariachi and other traditional forms; it also carries a lot of the most popular NPR programs.

SERVICES
Banks

Banks are plentiful, and grocery stores and pharmacies increasingly have ATMs inside. Downtown, look for **New Mexico Bank &** **Trust** (320 Gold Ave. SW, 505/830-8100, 9 A.M.–4 P.M. Mon.–Thurs., 9 A.M.–5 P.M. Fri.). In Nob Hill, **Wells Fargo** is on Central at Dartmouth (3022 Central Ave. SE, 505/255-4372, 9 A.M.–5 P.M. Mon.–Thurs., 9 A.M.–6 P.M. Fri., 9 A.M.–1 P.M. Sat.). Both have 24-hour ATMs.

Post Offices

Most convenient for visitors are the **Old Town Plaza Station** (303 Romero St. NW, 505/242-5927, 11 A.M.–4 P.M. Mon.–Fri., noon–3 P.M. Sat.), **Downtown Station** (201 5th St. SW, 505/346-1256, 9 A.M.–4:30 P.M. Mon.–Fri.), and an office near UNM (115 Cornell Dr. SE, 505/346-0923, 8 A.M.–5 P.M. Mon.–Fri.).

Internet

The main branch of the **Albuquerque Public Library** (501 Copper Ave. NW, 505/768-5141, www.cabq.gov/library, 10 A.M.–6 P.M. Mon. and Thurs.–Sat., 10 A.M.–7 P.M. Tues. and Wed.) offers Internet access with the one-time purchase of a $3 card that's good for three months for out-of-towners; wireless access is free. City-maintained wireless hotspots are listed at www.cabq.gov/wifi; many businesses around town also provide the service.

Getting There and Around

BY AIR

Albuquerque International Sunport (ABQ, 505/244-7700, www.cabq.gov/airport) is a pleasant single-terminal airport served by all of the major U.S. airlines. It's on the south side of the city, just east of I-25, about four miles from downtown. There's free wireless Internet access throughout the complex. Near baggage claim, you'll find a desk maintained by the convention and visitors bureau.

From the airport, there are three buses, all of which leave from the far west end of the terminal, on the arrivals level. The city ABQ Ride bus Route 50 ($1) runs from the airport to the main bus hub, the Alvarado Transportation Center at Central and 2nd Street downtown. Buses depart every half hour 7 A.M.–8 P.M., and on Saturdays every hour and 10 minutes 9:45 A.M.–7:05 P.M.; there is no Sunday service. The ride takes about 25 minutes. On weekdays, there's also a free express shuttle (Route 250) to the same stop downtown, with four departures (9:10 A.M.–6:17 P.M.) timed to meet the commuter train to Santa Fe; the ride takes 15 minutes. One other weekday-only bus (Route 222, $1)) runs to the nearest commuter train stop, just 15 minutes away; departures are four times a day. Verify the latter two schedules online at www.nmrailrunner.com, as the train schedule can change.

BY CAR

All of the major car-rental companies have offices in a single convenient complex adjacent to the airport, connected by shuttle buses. **Hertz** and **Enterprise** offer service at the Amtrak depot (really just a refund for the cab ride to the airport offices), and Hertz has two other locations around town—sometimes less expensive because you bypass the airport service fee. (If you're up for a public-transit adventure right off the plane, you could potentially get from the airport to the San Mateo Hertz office on the city bus, Route 222 eastbound, then Route 141; it takes about an hour.)

BY BUS

Greyhound (800/231-2222, www.greyhound. com) runs buses from all major points east, west, north, and south, though departures are not frequent. The bus station (320 1st St. SW, 505/243-4435) is just south of the Alvarado Transportation Center. Cheaper *and* nicer are the bus services that cater to Mexicans traveling across the Southwest and into Mexico, though they offer service only to Santa Fe and Las Cruces; **El Paso-Los Angeles Limousine Express** (1611 Central Ave. SW, 505/247-8036, www.eplalimo.com) is the biggest operator.

With **ABQ Ride** (505/243-7433, www.cabq. gov/transit) public buses, it's possible to reach all of the major sights along Central Avenue,

but you can't get to the Sandia Peak Tramway or anywhere in the east mountains.

The most tourist-friendly bus is Route 66, the one that runs along Central Avenue, linking Old Town, downtown, and Nob Hill; service runs until 1 A.M. on summer weekends. The double-length red **Rapid Ride** buses (Route 766) follow the same route but stop at only the most popular stops. The fare for all buses, regardless of trip length, is $1; **passes** are available for one ($2), two ($4), and three ($6) days and can be purchased on the bus.

BY TRAIN

Amtrak (800/USA-RAIL, www.amtrak.com) runs the Southwest Chief through Albuquerque, arriving daily in the afternoon from Chicago and Los Angeles. The depot shares space with the Greyhound terminal, downtown on 1st Street, south of Central Avenue and the Alvarado Transportation Center.

The **Rail Runner** (866/795-RAIL, www. nmrailrunner.com) runs from downtown Santa Fe through Albuquerque and as far south as Belén. The main stop in Albuquerque is the downtown Alvarado Transportation Center, at Central and 1st Street. It's fantastic service to or from Santa Fe, but within Albuquerque, the system doesn't go anywhere visitors typically go. If you ride, keep your ticket—you get a free transfer from the train to any city bus.

www.moon.com

DESTINATIONS | ACTIVITIES | BLOGS | MAPS | BOOKS

MOON.COM is ready to help plan your next trip! Filled with fresh trip ideas and strategies, author interviews, informative travel blogs, a detailed map library, and descriptions of all the Moon guidebooks, Moon.com is all you need to get out and explore the world—or even places in your own backyard. While at Moon.com, sign up for our monthly e-newsletter for updates on new releases, travel tips, and expert advice from our on-the-go Moon authors. As always, when you travel with Moon, expect an experience that is uncommon and truly unique.

KEEP UP WITH MOON ON FACEBOOK AND TWITTER
JOIN THE MOON PHOTO GROUP ON FLICKR

MAP SYMBOLS

▦	Expressway	🄲	Highlight	✈	Airport	⚲	Golf Course
	Primary Road	○	City/Town	✗	Airfield	🄿	Parking Area
	Secondary Road	◉	State Capital	▲	Mountain	▰	Archaeological Site
	Unpaved Road	✪	National Capital	✛	Unique Natural Feature	⛪	Church
	Trail	★	Point of Interest				
	Ferry	•	Accommodation	🕊	Waterfall	⛽	Gas Station
	Railroad	▼	Restaurant/Bar	▲	Park	◯	Glacier
	Pedestrian Walkway	■	Other Location	🄾	Trailhead		Mangrove
	Stairs	⋀	Campground	⛷	Skiing Area		Reef
							Swamp

CONVERSION TABLES

°C = (°F - 32) / 1.8
°F = (°C x 1.8) + 32
1 inch = 2.54 centimeters (cm)
1 foot = 0.304 meters (m)
1 yard = 0.914 meters
1 mile = 1.6093 kilometers (km)
1 km = 0.6214 miles
1 fathom = 1.8288 m
1 chain = 20.1168 m
1 furlong = 201.168 m
1 acre = 0.4047 hectares
1 sq km = 100 hectares
1 sq mile = 2.59 square km
1 ounce = 28.35 grams
1 pound = 0.4536 kilograms
1 short ton = 0.90718 metric ton
1 short ton = 2,000 pounds
1 long ton = 1.016 metric tons
1 long ton = 2,240 pounds
1 metric ton = 1,000 kilograms
1 quart = 0.94635 liters
1 US gallon = 3.7854 liters
1 Imperial gallon = 4.5459 liters
1 nautical mile = 1.852 km

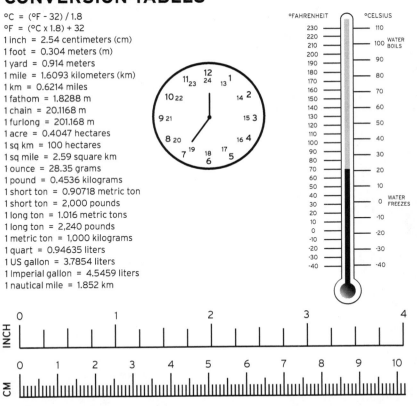

MOON SPOTLIGHT ALBUQUERQUE

Avalon Travel
a member of the Perseus Books Group
1700 Fourth Street
Berkeley, CA 94710, USA
www.moon.com

Editor: Jamie Andrade
Series Manager: Kathryn Ettinger
Copy Editor: Angela Buckley
Graphics Coordinators: Darren Alessi,
  Kathryn Osgood
Production Coordinators: Darren Alessi,
  Christine DeLorenzo
Cover Designer: Darren Alessi
Map Editor: Albert Angulo
Cartographers: Chris Henrick, Kat Bennett,
  Kaitlin Jaffe, and Albert Angulo

ISBN: 978-1-61238-604-1

Text © 2013 by Zora O'Neill.
Maps © 2013 by Avalon Travel.
All rights reserved.

Printed in the United States

ABOUT THE AUTHOR

Zora O'Neill

Zora O'Neill has lived in New York City since 1998, but still calls New Mexico home. Growing up, she attended ceremonial dances at Taos Pueblo and camped in the Pecos Wilderness – but she took it for granted, and perhaps even complained about it when she was dragged out of bed before dawn for some adventure. It wasn't until she had moved away and traveled the world that she realized in what a wild, culturally rich place she'd been raised.

Zora's travels and writing have taken her on a circuitous route back to her home. Graduate study in the Middle East taught her about the Arab roots of adobe and irrigation channels; visiting hotels in southern Spain while researching guidebooks was disorienting – the brick floors, thick walls, and shady courtyards felt just like those in Santa Fe. For guidebook work in Mexico, she has followed the threads of Spanish and indigenous culinary traditions as they made their way up to her home state.

All along in her travels, Zora has been particularly interested in food, occasionally working as a cook, caterer, and cookbook author (*Forking Fantastic! Put the Party Back in Dinner Party* was published in 2009). Working on this book gave her another excuse to seek out the best red chile enchiladas and most creative uses of local organic produce. She maintains a blog about her cooking, travel, and guidebook-research experiences at www.rovinggastronome. com. She also maintains an update website for this book, www. moonsantafe.com, where you can find out what has changed since publication. Zora is also the author of *Moon New Mexico*. She welcomes email from readers at zora@rovinggastronome.com.